D1640890

To my wife Dolores, for her unlimited
support in this adventure.

To my daughters, for their patience: they waited
for me during 64 days and 500 nights.

To Captain Robert FitzRoy:
we owe this story to him.

"The voyage of the Beagle has been by far the most important event in my life, and has determined my whole career"

Charles Darwin, August 3rd, 1876

Rhea Darwinii.

Charles Darwin
at southern south

On his tracks two centuries later

Presented by:

Charles Darwin
at southern south

With the sponsorship of:

Staff

Idea, photography & edition
Henry von Wartenberg

Texts
The Complete Work of Charles Darwin Online

Comment
Henry von Wartenberg

Art Director
Juan José Gómez

Translation
Andrea Schenone

Revision
Dolores Paillot

Additional historic work
Gerardo Bartolomé

Logistic support
Guillermo Rodríguez

Maps
Fernando San Martín

Executive production
TRIPLEVE EDITORES

Darwin's text & pictures reproduced with permission from John van Wyhe ed., The Complete Work of Charles Darwin Online http://darwin-online.org.uk/

Copyright 2010©Henry von Wartenberg

Von Wartenberg, Henry
   Charles Darwin, At Southern south / Henry von Wartenberg y Charles Darwin; edición literaria a cargo de Henry Wartenberg. - 1a ed. - Tigre : Tripleve Editores, 2010.
   240 p. ; 24x25 cm.

   Traducido por: Henry von Wartenberg
   ISBN 978-987-25379-2-0

   1. Relatos de Viajes. I. Darwin, Charles II. Von Wartenberg, Henry, ed. lit. III. Von Wartenberg, Henry, trad. IV. Título
   CDD 910.4

Graphics and maps included in this edition are only illustrative. They are not in scale, and do not committ in anyway the borders of Argentina, Chile and Uruguay.

The crew

"We had on board, when the Beagle sailed from England, seventy-four persons, namely:

Robert FitzRoy	Commander and Surveyor
John Clements Wickham	Lieutenant
Bartholomew James Sulivan	Lieutenant
Edward Main Chaffers	Master
Robert Mac-Cormick	Surgeon
George Rowlett	Purser
Alexander Derbishire	Mate
Peter Benson Stewart	Mate
John Lort Stokes	Mate and Assistant Surveyor
Benjamin Bynoe	Assistant Surgeon
Arthur Mellersh	Midshipman
Philip Gidley King	Midshipman
Alexander Burns Usborne	Master's Assistant
Charles Musters	Volunteer 1st Class
Jonathan May	Carpenter
Edward H. Hellyer	Clerk

On the list of supernumeraries were:

Charles Darwin	Naturalist
Augustus Earle	Draughtsman**
George James Stebbing	Instrument Maker

Richard Matthews and three Fuegians***: my own steward: and Mr. Darwin's servant. Acting boatswain: Sergeant of marines and seven privates: thirty-four seamen and six boys."

**The disappointment caused by losing his services was diminished by meeting Mr Conrad Martens at Monte Video, and engaging him to embark with me as my draughtsman.
***Fuegia Basket, Jemmy Button and York Minster

Captain Robert FitzRoy
H.M.S. Beagle

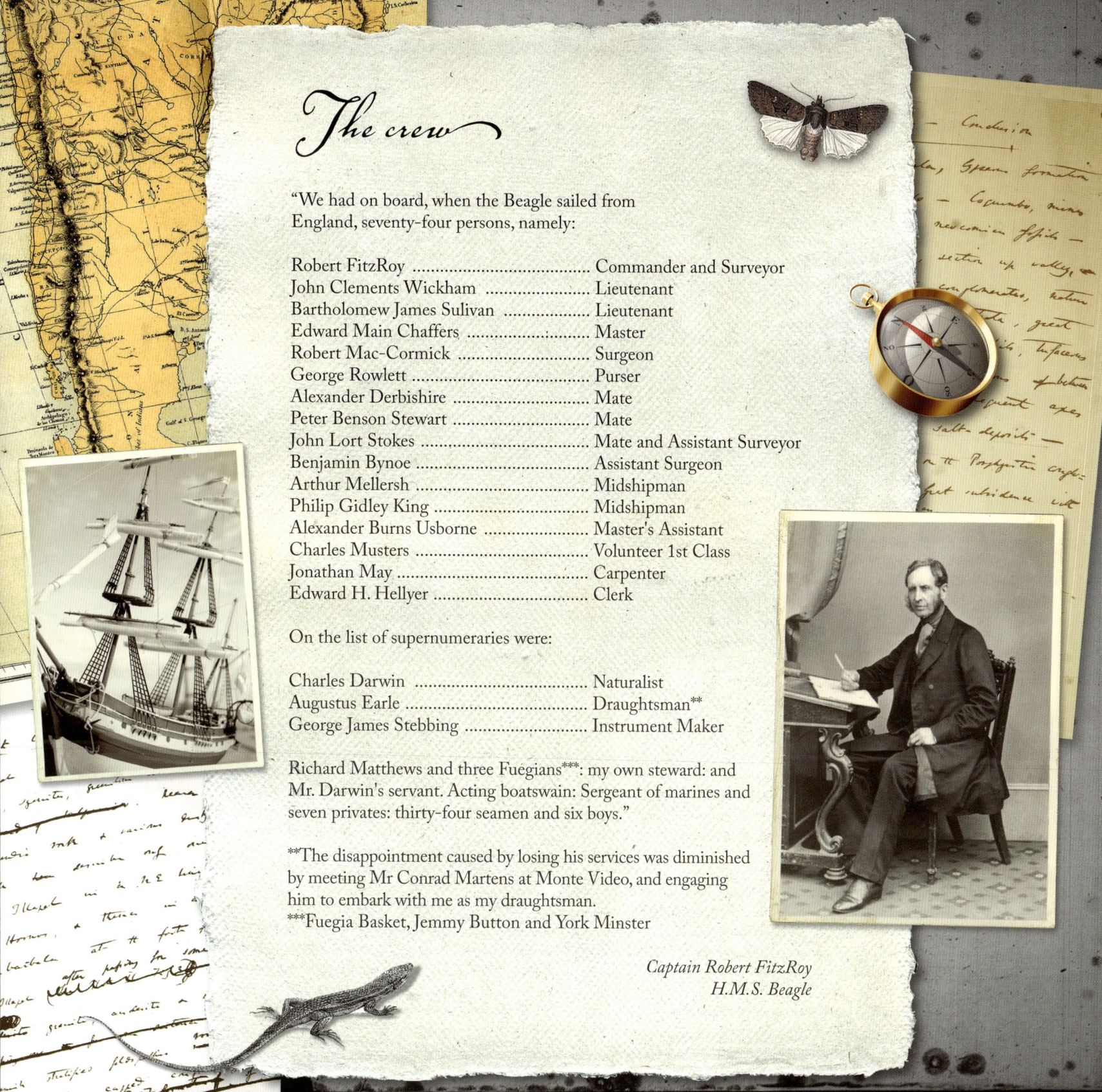

Index

Another Unstoppable GS	12
To the South of the South, 16 thousand kilometers after	14
Sailing towards glory	16
FitzRoy, the mentor of Charles Darwin	22
The H.M.S. Beagle: heading South of the South	24
Charles Darwin in Uruguay	26
From Montevideo to Maldonado	28
From Maldonado to Minas	32
Santa Fé City	76
Entre Ríos yesterday	78
Dodging jaguars in the Paraná River	80
And now... Tigre	82
Back in Uruguay	84
Charles Darwin in Carmelo & Punta Gorda	86
On the way to Patagonia	90
H.M.S. Beagle in Port Desire	92
H.M.S. Beagle in San Julián	96
Expedition to Santa Cruz River	104
Good Success Bay in Tierra del Fuego	113

Centenary olive trees	36
To Patagonia we steer	38
A long horseback ride on wild territories	40
Charles Darwin and Juan Manuel de Rosas	42
Between Colorado River and Bahía Blanca	46
The origin of On The Origin of Species?	48
South American ostrich	52
On the way to Buenos Aires	54
Charles Darwin in Buenos Aires	62
From Buenos Aires to Santa Fé	68
Charles Darwin and José de San Martín	72

1832-2010	116
Cape Horn	118
A BMW F 800GS at the end of the world	122
Navarino Island and the Fuegians	124
Woollya	128
Navarino Island today	132
Following Darwin to Tarn Mount	134
Strait of Magellan	138
San Isidro's Lighthouse	142

On trip to Luján de Cuyo	206
Charles Darwin in Villa Vicencio	210
Paramillos Petrified Woods	214
Las Vacas River	218
Incas Bridge	222
Valley of the Aconcagua	224
Leaving the Cordillera behind	228
Returning to England	230
Back home	232
FitzRoy, Darwin & Napoleón	236
Bibliography	238
Acknowledgements	240

The Fuegian Channels	152
Central Chile	158
Valparaíso Surroundings	164
Ascent to La Campana Mount	166
Cauquenes Hotbaths	171
Yaquil Mines	174
Chiloé and Chonos Islands	178
Valdivia & Niebla Fort	186
Earthquake in Valdivia, Concepción & Talcahuano	190
Crossing the Cordillera	196
Darwin in Mendoza	200

Another Unstoppable GS

When we first met Henry von Wartenberg and he told us about his idea of going on this trip, we felt immediately motivated to somehow support this exciting adventure.

We looked at different alternatives and, of course, the one that came up right away was that of providing him with the necessary mobility to reach all the different places along this extensive trip through Argentina, Chile and Uruguay following the path of the famous English naturalist Charles Darwin.

We immediately thought that nothing could be more appropriate than a motorcycle, especially considering the rough geography of some areas Henry would cover. The BMW F 800 GS also came to mind as a good option. Considering how well it adapts to different terrains and its ideal weight, this bike would make an excellent partner for his trip.

Since the early 20th century, BMW's name has been linked to big trips, adventures and all kinds of feats. Important men accompanied by the value and support of our product's technology have achieved great objectives. Mobility coupled with the spirit of adventure has always driven men not only to beat new records but to explore the world connecting different cultures and somehow shortening distances. In 1932, aviation pioneer Wolfang von Gronau covered 45.000 kilometers on a successful first attempt round-the world flight on a large flying boat equipped with BMW engines. As early as then, BMW has been providing the reliability of its products to shorten the distance between far-away places through something as important as mobility.

Since then to our days we could mention many men, who, with the same entrepreneurial spirit as Henry von Wartenberg and with a will to improve themselves, have been able to set important records together with the mobility enabled by our technology.

That is why we did not hesitate to support Henry, who in the 21st century decided to explore in his own way and capture with his camera the places traveled by Darwin 200 years ago although certainly with far more logistical difficulties. I believe it would be fair to say that both Charles Darwin and Henry von Wartenberg would have "envied" certain aspects of each other's worlds. In the case of Charles Darwin maybe the advances of technology, Henry would probably have liked to be able to visit those places for the first time as a privileged adventurer.

Beyond all comparisons, we believe that there is something they will both share forever, namely the majesty of the places they traveled to, immortalized in Darwin's work and becoming the centerpiece of his theories, and in Henry's case immortalized by the amazing talent of the photographer who knows how to capture the soul of what lies behind the lens. The captivating landscapes of these three countries will also certainly help.

We are proud of having been able to make our small contribution to this invaluable project and we are convinced that it will also serve as inspiration to more than one person eager to fulfill their dreams or set out on that trip or exploration they have longed for.

Books have been a source of inspiration to millions through the ages. Besides the stories, the images of this trip will for sure remain in the memory of all its readers. ∎

Alejandro Echeagaray
BMW Group Argentina

To the South of the South, 16 thousand kilometers after

By Henry von Wartenberg

One May afternoon in the year 2009, while I was visiting bookstores to check on how my books were selling, I asked the owner of "Cinco Esquinas" to recommend any biography on Charles Darwin. Without hesitating, Analuz stretched her arm towards a shelf and gave me a little green book that said DARWIN in capital letters and had a smaller yet eye-catching subtitle that read: The story of an extraordinary man. The author, Tim Berra, is an Ohio State University professor.

This book narrates, in a dynamic and precise way, the life of this English Naturalist and highlights transcendental aspects, but in a telegraphic version, of certain events. This is understandable, if one is to account for the adventures of a restless man in one hundred and forty pages of a pocket book.

My greatest curiosity had to do with his expedition on board the Beagle in South America, sailing under captain FitzRoy, forerunner of everything to come.

This is how I started reading other texts as well: his travelling journals, FitzRoy's narrations, *The Voyage of the H.M.S. Beagle*, edited by The Folio Society that compiles and crosses the protagonists' first letters and log books; the novel *This Thing of Darkness* by Harry Thompson and other books that have filled my library. I have spent whole afternoons sitting near the fireplace surrounded by old and new maps, googling names, places and other data. Many times, I have also consulted my favourite photographic files, since I had been in many of the places described by these adventurers. I didn't take long to realize the book I could create with this story. Luckily, partners like BMW and Fundación YPF didn't take long to show up and embrace my proposal, and were later on joined by La Caja, Cruceros Australis, Rev'it! and Casa Chic.

This project entailed significant logistics, for we had to travel to remote places and fulfill the historic rigor in terms of geographical accuracy. Those familiar with my other books know of my passion for motorbikes, which, in this case, proved to be the ideal means of transportation for this tour. Darwin covered so much territory on a horse…and what is a motorbike but a modern horse?

I drove 14.663 kilometers through three different countries during two months. I crossed plains, brooks and woods. I climbed Mount Tarn all on my own, and many times, during inland excursions I had the feeling that if anything happened to me no one would ever find me. I sailed the southern channels in different vessels (even with my bike on board one time). I visited Bahía del Buen Suceso on an Argentine Armada ship and was lucky to disembark in Cape Horn on the Via Australis cruise. During the journey I spoke before schools and half a dozen other audiences and met charming people who facilitated my work.

A recurrent question was when I was planning to visit the Galapagos Islands. "Not on this trip!" was always my answer. In the same way the name Maradona is worldly associated with Argentina, so is the name Darwin to the Galápagos Islands. Though in this case it is not so. I've got nothing against this famous island; moreover, I'd love to visit it some time, but the truth is that throughout Darwin's journey,

Galápagos was just another stop for the *Beagle*. This stop lasted four weeks and its aim was the refueling of water and turtle meat (they travelled alive) and most of the time was spent drawing maps. It was during this stop that Darwin confirmed some of his important ideas.

This voyage through Argentina, Chile and Uruguay lasted three years! Darwin collected fossils, geological specimens and gained knowledge that would later become the basis of his theory on the evolution of species.

His book *On The Origin of Species* was conceived in these lands. When in San Julián Port, in January 1834, and after finding a complete fossil of an animal related to a *guanaco*, the giant *Macrauchenia*, Darwin wrote:

"*It is impossible to reflect upon the change that has taken place in the American continent without a feeling of awe. In ancient times, America must have been a melting pot of big monsters; nowadays, we can only find pigmies, if compared to their preceding races.*"

He tried out answers for the same questions during his stay in Punta Alta and Bahía Blanca, and confirmed his suspicions regarding the origin of the Andes after crossing them through various places. He challenged beliefs and returned to England with the raw material to build a solid career.

Despite controversies, he was highly respected and admired during his last years. He is buried in Westminster Abbey, surrounded by kings and other personalities such as Isaac Newton and the explorer David Livingstone.

I invite you to relive this voyage, celebrating 178 years of his arrival in Montevideo on board the *H.M.S. Beagle*. I encourage you to compare his past descriptions to my present photographs. This is the aim of this book. Something like the evolution of the evolution Charles once posed.

And why not pay a small tribute to captain FitzRoy, the one and only responsible for making Darwin visit these lands. Though contrary in nature, one being a creator, the other, an evolutionist, the first a tory, the other a whig, they shared one of the most extraordinary adventures of all times. ∎

Sailing towards glory

By Gerardo Bartolomé

In 1831 a young man in his early twenties and lacking of a professional orientation started a trip that would change the way we see the World, Man and even God. His experience in South America filled Charles Darwin with doubts and beliefs that would be crucial when, many years later, he developed his (r)evolutionary ideas.

But… who was Darwin? A traveller that described a world that no longer exists? A naturalist who discovered dozens of species? A geologist who understood the way this continent was shaped? Or a scientist who formulated the Theory of Evolution? Charles Darwin was all of this.

DARWIN BEFORE BEING DARWIN. Charles Darwin was born in a wealthy family. His mother, Susannah Wedgewood, one of the owners of the famous Wedgewood pottery, died when he was just a boy and was consequently raised by his sisters.

Robert, his distant father, decided that Charles must be a physician like him, and sent him to study medicine at the University of Edinburgh. After a year he returned defeated. He could not stand working with blood and patients. His father became very angry, he could not accept the idea of having an idle son only dedicated to hunting and social meetings; so Robert decided that if his son didn't have a professional inclination then he would become a clergyman. Luckily Charles was sent to Cambridge to complete a general university education; he had two years to find an orientation, if not… the Church.

But how was it that this disoriented young Englishman became an explorer of the South American region?

THE VOYAGE THAT ALMOST DID NOT HAPPEN. In the meantime, in the remote Tierra del Fuego, the young English Captain Robert FitzRoy commanded H.M.S. Beagle. He surveyed channels connecting the Atlantic and Pacific oceans so that British ships could safely sail from England to the new colonies in Australia.

When back in England the ambitious FitzRoy was already planning his next voyage to improve even more his maps. He equipped the famous ship with the most recent scientific inventions like lightning rods affixed on every mast and twenty two chronometers to be able to calculate the most accurate coordinates ever before. It was also his initiative the creation of a new position,

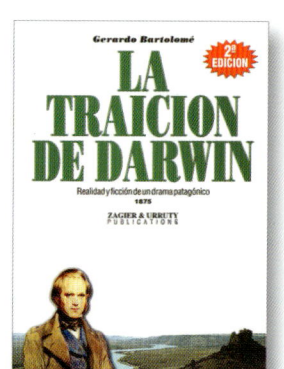

Gerardo Bartolomé, escritor de novelas históricas, es autor de "La traición de Darwin" y más recientemente de "El límite de la mentiras", una biografía del Perito Moreno.

H.M.S. Beagle painted by Pablo Pereyra for this book.

the onboard naturalist, to thoroughly and scientifically describe the unexplored lands. A young Cambridge botany professor was recommended to him, John Henslow, but he declined the invitation for he could not leave his wife and children for so long. The professor indicated his favourite student as suitable for the position: Charles Darwin.

At first FitzRoy was not pleased by Darwin, he did not have scientific experience and his personality was too introverted. But later, maybe because he didn't find anybody better qualified, the captain accepted Charles. Robert Darwin did not give his authorization for his son's trip, he was sure that the young man was escaping from his responsibilities. Luckily uncle Josiah Wedgewood wrote a convincing letter on Charles´ behalf and he received his father's consent.

"To Glory we steer!" shouted FitzRoy from the command bridge as the Beagle set sail from Devonport on the morning of December 27th 1831.

MORE THAN JUST A VOYAGE. H.M.S. Beagle was 28 metres long, had a beam of 7,5 mts, a draught of 3,8 mts and a crew of 74 people. It would not only survey Tierra del Fuego but also natural harbours along the Patagonian coast where damaged ships could be repaired after the daunting crossing of the Magellan Strait. Finally they would return to England across the Pacific Ocean, completing the circumnavigation.

Surveying the infamous fuegian channels was only possible during summer, so the rest of the year they would survey the Patagonian coast and would restock the ship in Buenos Aires and Montevideo. Thus, the voyage would take five years long.

Onboard Charles led a busy life. He slept on a hammock over the maps table, along with other young officials; he had

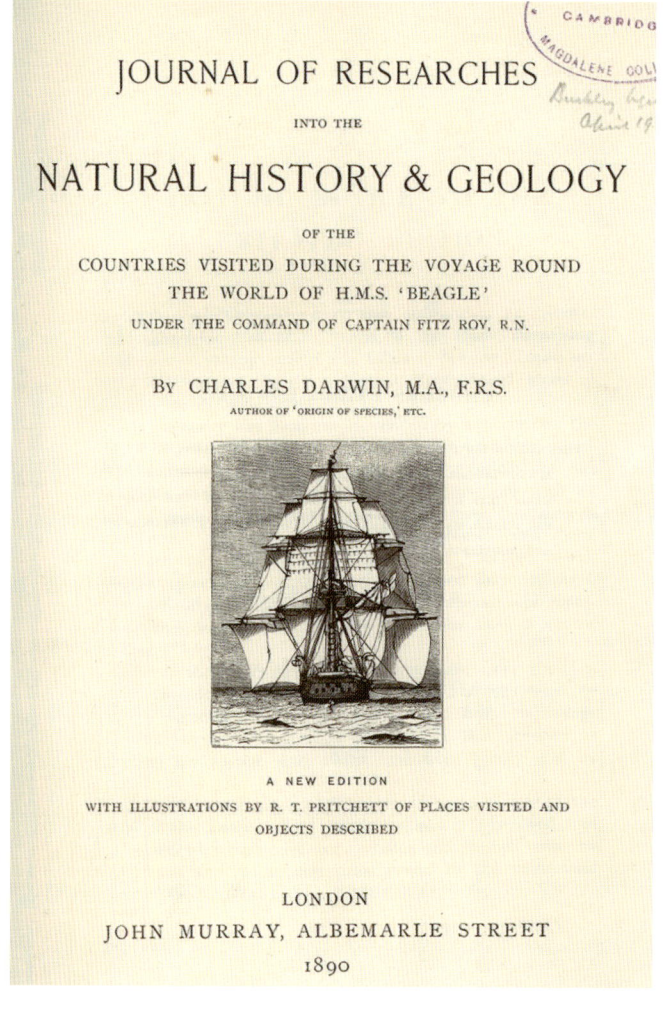

breakfast in the captain's cabin where they talked about the Naturalist's work; he catalogued and packed the animal and plant species he collected; he wrote a diary with the detailed description of his work and experiences and wrote letters for his family. On every harbour they would send to England the correspondence and Darwin's packages. Every now and then he received books to complete his scientific education.

Whenever possible Charles left the ship for he preferred

land expeditions. He crossed the "pampas" while the Governor of Buenos Aires was engaged in a war against the Indians, he bordered the Paraná River from Buenos Aires to Santa Fé, he rode through Uruguay, he crossed the Andes, he walked the island of Chiloé, he explored Chile from Valparaiso to Coquimbo, and together with FitzRoy he surveyed the Santa Cruz River crossing all of the Patagonia till just a few hours walking from Lake Argentino, thus losing the possibility of discovering it. Onboard the Beagle he visited and surveyed Patagonian harbours such as: Puerto Deseado, San Julián and Puerto Santa Cruz. In Tierra del Fuego FitzRoy and Darwin sailed the maze of channels, the captain naming most of the prominent places with the names of his crew. That's how Tierra del Fuego's highest mountain became Mount Darwin.

DISTURBING DISCOVERIES. In those days the biblical version of the Creation was not questioned; not even scientists, with very few exceptions, had any doubts. Few weeks after departing Darwin made interesting observations regarding the geology of certain islands in the Atlantic Ocean. Contrary to the Bible he thought that they had emerged from the bottom of the sea. So when he arrived to Argentina he believed in a changing world and not in the Bible any more.

Darwin's most interesting discovery, onboard the Beagle, happened on September 22nd of 1832 on the gravel cliffs by the sea near Punta Alta. His digging exposed bones that seemed to be part of an enormous unknown animal. Fossils, that's what these bones were, were already known by science but nobody really knew what they meant. Many thought that they were a fraud created by those who found them. Charles immediately understood that fossils were the key to the "mystery of mysteries", as he called the origin of Man and other species. He deduced that they belonged to extinct animals. Darwin found fossils all along the Argentine territory: in Punta Alta a megatherium, a sort of giant sloth –on the banks of the Salado River a glyptodon, a giant armadillo– in the gravel cliffs by the Paraná River a tooth of a pre-Columbian horse –in San Julián a macrauquenia,

In the shores of Patagonia Charles could also read signs of a changing world. He found oyster fossils by the coast, but he also found many more miles away from the sea and hundreds of metres above the sea level. The Naturalist deduced that the Patagonian coast was being elevated from the sea bottom. But it was not only the Patagonian coast …

The Beagle arrived to the Chilean harbour of Talcahuano just a few days after a devastating earthquake. By the shore Darwin found recently dead muscles about one metre above sea level. He deduced that the earthquake had elevated the land one metre and maybe, over the span of millions of years, the same earthquakes had created the Andes. To prove it, when the Beagle anchored at Valparaíso, Darwin left for a land expedition across the Andes. If he was right he had to find sea fossils over the mountains. And he did, almost four thousand metres high!

resembling a guanaco– and many others: mastodons, toxodons, etc. Darwin wrote in his diary "We may conclude that the whole area of the Pampas is one wide sepulchre of these extinct gigantic quadrupeds". But why are extinct animals so similar to living ones? The answer was the beginning of the idea of the evolution of species.

He later made another finding in the same direction. He discovered that there were two different American rheas: one, the well known ñandú or rhea of the Pampas, but he found another one, a Patagonian rhea (choique) which he called "avestruz petise". He also observed many diferent armadillo species living in the same region. Closely allied species living in nearby regions suggested him a common past. The concept of what we now call Biogeography was developed by Darwin in Argentina and it became one of the pillars of the Theory of Evolution.

MAN, ANOTHER ANIMAL. The Fuegian indians caused Charles great impression. On December 18th, 1832 he wrote: "I would not have believed how entire the difference between savage and civilized man is". The Fuegians seemed to live in a "savage" state similar to that of man before civilization. Darwin had met "civilized" Fuegians since FitzRoy had taken in his previous trip three of them to be educated in London and were now returning onboard the Beagle to their land. Thus Darwin understood the enormous impact that education has on human behaviour and deduced that, without any trace of civilization, Man would not be much different from other animals. When, many years later, he applied the concepts of animal evolution on Man he deduced the origin of our specie. This was the basis of his most controversial book: "The Descent of Man".

It was also from the Fuegians that he obtained another of the keys to his theories. Jemmy Button, one of FitzRoy's "civilized" Indians, told him that during famine times his tribe (Yahgans) had to fight against a rival tribe, the Onas, for survival. Years later, when reading Malthus, he recalled Jemmy´s comments and deduced that animals, the same as savage Man, battle for the means of survival. This is the concept of Natural Selection: the engine that moves Evolution.

AT HOME. When the surveying was finished in 1835 the Beagle set sail to Europe across the Pacific Ocean. In the Galapagos Islands they restocked their supply of fresh water and meat from giant tortoises. There Darwin found more evidence supporting the ideas of Biogeography that he had developed in Patagonia. When he arrived in England Charles was already convinced of the evolution of species and the origin of Man, but why did it take him twenty three years to publish them?

In Great Britain Darwin led a quiet life. He married his cousin Emma Wedgewood and had many children. He bought a big house south of London; together with FitzRoy he published the memoirs of the voyage and dedicated his time to the study of hundreds of species that he had collected. Most probably, knowing that his ideas were contrary to the Bible, Charles felt that their disclosure would have a great impact on the British society, affecting his family; so he decided to give his "evolutionist" writings to his editor with instructions of publication only once he and Emma were dead.

Many years later Darwin received a letter from a young Englishman living in Malaysia: Alfred Wallace. He asked Darwin to read the attached essay on Malaysian butterflies and have it published if he found it worthy. Darwin immediately understood that Wallace's work contained the same fundamentals of evolution that he had developed many years before. He would lose the authorship of "his" theory. Truly depressed he sent the writing to scientist friends of his, but since they already knew Darwin's ideas they presented, together with Wallace´s essay, some of Darwin´s old letters on the same subject. Since there were no negative repercussions Darwin decided to publish, in 1859, his memorable "On The Origin of Species". That did unleash a great debate between Church and scientists.

In 1865 Darwin went a step further and published "The Descent of Man", where he exposed the origin of the humans, increasing the debate in the society.

After his death, on April 19th 1882, further scientific discoveries confirmed Darwin's ideas. Even though many people still discuss "Evolution vs. Creation", scientists agree on Darwin and his theory is the basis of Biology and modern Medicine.

Now, almost 180 years after his visit to South America, his observations have great importance because their accuracy allows us to imagine how this region looked like before the arrival of civilization. I followed his footsteps to write my novel "Darwin's Betrayal" ("La traición de Darwin") and now Henry von Wartenberg presents us pictures that invite to visit this awesome part of our continent. ∎

Fitz Roy
the mentor of Charles Darwin

"Anxious that no opportunity of collecting useful information during the voyage should be lost; I proposed to the Hydrographer that some well-educated and scientific person should be sought for who would willingly share such accommodations as I had to offer, in order to profit by the opportunity of visiting distant countries yet little known. Captain Beaufort approved of the suggestion, and wrote to Professor Peacock, of Cambridge, who consulted with a friend, Professor Henslow, and he named Mr. Charles Darwin, grandson of Dr. Darwin the poet, as a young man of promising ability, extremely fond of geology, and indeed all branches of natural history. In consequence an offer was made to Mr. Darwin to be my guest on board, which he accepted conditionally; permission was obtained for his embarkation, and an order given by the Admiralty that he should be borne on the ship's books for provisions. The conditions asked by Mr. Darwin were, that he should be at liberty to leave the Beagle and retire from the Expedition when he thought proper, and that he should pay a fair share of the expenses of my table."

This is how Captain FitzRoy told in his book *Narratives* the reason why Darwin embarked the H.M.S. Beagle. It was not an easy decision for the promising naturalist. In fact he had to overcome some obstacles: he broke the promise he had made to his father of becoming an Anglican minister after graduating from Cambridge.

But the opportunity of his life was in front of him, in FitzRoy's hands.

Not only the Captain's choice of taking Darwin was smart... You just have to oversee the notes of the ship log (in the photograph on the right) to appreciate the commitment and full dedication assumed by the young commander –only a few years older than Darwin– during the mission.

The log is now in Argentina, a historic jewel, part of the permanent collection of the Museo Naval de la Armada. It was bought in an auction at Sotheby's during the forties for 270 pounds. All the records of the voyage from 1833 until 1836 are on its pages. ■

H.M.S. Beagle: heading South of the South

July 5th, 1832

"In the morning we got under way, and stood out of the splendid harbour of Rio de Janeiro. In our passage to the Plata, we saw nothing particular, excepting on one day a great shoal of porpoises, many hundreds in number. The whole sea was in places furrowed by them; and a most extraordinary spectacle was presented, as hundreds, proceeding together by jumps, in which their whole bodies were exposed, thus cut the water. (...) As soon as we entered the estuary of the Plata, the weather was very unsettled. One dark night we were surrounded by numerous seals and penguins, which made such strange noises.

When within the mouth of the river, I was interested by observing how slowly the waters of the sea and river mixed. The latter, muddy and discoloured, from its less specific gravity, floated on the surface of the salt water. This was curiously exhibited in the wake of the vessel, where a line of blue water was seen mingling in little eddies, with the adjoining fluid."

C.D.

The route

- Departure from Devonport, England: *December 27th, 1831*
- Montevideo: *July, 1832*
- Buenos Aires: *November, 1832*
- Bahía del Buen Suceso: *December of 1832/February of 1833*
- Cabo de Hornos: *December, 1832*
- Seno Goeree (Isla Navarino): *January, 1833*
- Islas Malvinas: *March, 1833*
- Mouth of Río Negro: *August, 1833*

- Tigre: *October 20th, 1833*
- Montevideo: *November 4th, 1833*
- Cufré: *November 15th, 1833*
- Colonia: *November 17th, 1833*
- Mercedes: *November 23rd, 1833*
- Montevideo: *November 28th, 1833*

- Puerto Deseado: *December 23rd, 1833*
- Puerto San Julián: *January 9th, 1834*
- Estrecho de Magallanes, Isla Elizabeth: *January 30th, 1834*
- Islas Woollaston: *February 25th, 1834*
- Río Santa Cruz: *April 13th, 1834*

- Estrecho de Magallanes, Bahía Gregorio: *May 29th, 1834*
- Puerto Hambre: *June 1st, 1834*
- Canal Magdalena: *June, 1834*
- Isla de Chiloé: *July, 1834*
- Santiago: *August, 1834*
- Rancagua: *September, 1834*
- Archipiélago de Chonos: *December, 1834*
- Valparaíso: *November, 1834*
- Valdivia: *February, 1835*
- Concepción: *March, 1835*
- Santiago: *March, 1835*

Charles Darwin in Uruguay

July 26th, 1832

"We anchored at Monte Video. The Beagle was employed in surveying the extreme southern and eastern coasts of America, south of the Plata, during the two succeeding years. To prevent useless repetitions, I will extract those parts of my journal which refer to the same districts, without always attending to the order in which we visited them."

C.D.

This succinct description of Charles Darwin on the passing of the H.M.S. Beagle through Montevideo is too brief for the events taking place on those days. The chronicles the English originally wrote are much more generous. They tell the story of their arrival on August 2nd, 1832 at the port of Buenos Aires where they were attacked by an Argentine ship in a confusing episode. This ship almost hit the rigs of the Beagle with its canon. After the immediate return to Montevideo, and after filing several complaints to the corresponding diplomats, they found themselves immersed in another war episode: a mutiny had broken out in the city between ex president Rivera's supporters and supporters of the then president, Lavalleja. Brasilian soldiers and those belonging to the united provinces were trying to profit from the situation by fighting for their causes. Moreover, black soldiers wanted to free slaves, possibly the only wise idea in such violent times.
The British consul and the chief of the local police turned to captain FitzRoy and his men to restore order and safeguard British subjects who lived in Montevideo. Both tasks were successfully achieved and maybe one of the most important movements was to take the fortress on the hill. This tower had many crew members of the Beagle as observers; Charles Darwin was amongst them.

from Montevideo to Maldonado

August, 1833

"Maldonado is situated on the northern bank of the Plata, and not very far from the mouth of the estuary. It is a most quiet, forlorn, little town; built, as is universally the case in these countries, with the streets running at right angles to each other, and having in the middle a large plaza or square, which, from its size, renders the scantiness of the population more evident. It possesses scarcely any trade (...)

The town is separated from the river by a band of sand-hillocks, about a mile broad: it is surrounded, on all other sides, by an open slightly-undulating country, covered by one uniform layer of fine green turf, on which countless herds of cattle, sheep, and horses graze.. (...)

I may mention, as a proof how cheap everything is in this country, that I paid only two dollars a day, or eight shillings, for two men, together with a troop of about a dozen riding-horses. My companions were well armed with pistols and sabres; a precaution which I thought rather unnecessary; but the first piece of news we heard was, that, the day before, a traveller from Monte Video had been found dead on the road, with his throat cut."

C.D.

Darwin toured Maldonado and its surroundings for two months and a half. He slept in a boarding house on Florida Street (Florida and Sarandí). Today, the town is not small anymore: it has more than 50 thousand residents and its city hall covers one of the wealthiest areas in Uruguay. Colonel (R) Daoiz Bonilla is one of those in charge of retelling its history. Punta del Este is a clear example of urban evolution. Founded in 1829 by Don Francisco Aguilar, it was at the beginning an indigenous settlement which later became a village for fishermen. Its first name was "Villa Ituzaingo", but in 1907 it gained its definite name: Punta del Este. It keeps on growing ever since, and today it is known as one of the most exclusive seaside resorts in South America.

Charles told of his trips outside Maldonado:

On the first night we slept at a retired little country-house; and there I soon found out that I possessed two or three articles, especially a pocket compass, which created unbounded astonishment. In every house I was asked to show the compass, and by its aid, together with a map, to point out the direction of various places. It excited the liveliest admiration that I, a perfect stranger, should know the road (for direction and road are synonymous in this open country) to places where I had never been. At one house a young woman, who was ill in bed, sent to entreat me to come and show her the compass. If their surprise was great, mine was greater, to find such ignorance among people who possessed their thousands of cattle, and "estancias" of great extent. (...)

I was asked whether the earth or sun moved; whether it was hotter or colder to the north; where Spain was, and many other such questions."

C.D.

If Darwin returned to Uruguay, his surprise would be enormous to see how it has changed in the last hundred years, especially in terms of education. These students from school Number 18 of Villa Darwin, in Soriano, are a faithful reflection of this. Although the school is far from the geography Charles previously mentions, it is an example of what education can do in a country with a strong policy on this issue.

from Maldonado to Minas

August, 1833

"Las Minas is much smaller even than Maldonado. It is seated on a little plain, and is surrounded by low rocky mountains. It is of the usual symmetrical form; and with its whitewashed church standing in the centre, had rather a pretty appearance. The outskirting houses rose out of the plain like isolated beings, without the accompaniment of gardens or courtyards. This is generally the case in the country, and all the houses have, in consequence, an uncomfortable aspect. At night we stopped at a pulpería, or drinking shop. During the evening a great number of Gauchos came in to drink spirits and smoke cigars: their appearance is very striking; they are generally tall and handsome. (...) They frequently wear their moustaches, and long black hair curling down their backs. Their politeness is excessive; they never drink their spirits without expecting you to taste it; but whilst making their exceedingly graceful bow, they seem quite as ready, if occasion offered, to cut your throat."

C.D.

The old route 12, that joins Laguna del Sauce with Minas is still a road with few traffic, but with a spectacular geography. It is the same road Darwin took two centuries ago.

The general, and almost entire absence of trees in Banda Oriental is remarkable. Some of the rocky hills are partly covered by thickets, and on the banks of the larger streams, especially to the north of Las Minas, willow-trees are not uncommon. Near the Arroyo Tapes I heard of a wood of palms; and one of these trees, of considerable size, I saw near the Pan de Azúcar, in lat. 35°. These, and the trees planted by the Spaniards, offer the only exceptions to the general scarcity of wood. Among the introduced kinds may be enumerated poplars, olives, peach, and other fruit trees: the peaches succeed so well, that they afford the main supply of firewood to the city of Buenos Ayres."

C.D.

Uruguay changed radically and the trees are so present in its physiognomy that it is hard to imagine a landscape without them. The consistent forest policy Uruguay has adopted in the last decades has had a profound impact in its present economy and generates important employment throughout the country.

Centenary olive trees

From the old species Darwin describes, peach trees are no longer used for wood; olive trees, on the contrary, have kept their force. In the area of Carmelo, more precisely in Punta Gorda, there is a wide variety of olive trees, amongst centenary and renewed trees, and its high quality oil production is a national pride for which International prizes have been awarded.

The warm May sun is trying to make its way behind the coronillas (crown vetches) in Punta Gorda. The end of the harvest of olives is drawing near, and the days during this season are shorter. We need to start early!

To Patagonia we steer

July 24th, 1833

"The Beagle sailed from Maldonado, and on August the 3rd she arrived off the mouth of the Rio Negro. This is the principal river on the whole line of coast between the Strait of Magellan and the Plata. It enters the sea about three hundred miles south of the estuary of the Plata. About fifty years ago, under the old Spanish government, a small colony was established here; and it is still the most southern position (lat. 41°) on this eastern coast of America, inhabited by civilized man.

The country near the mouth of the river is wretched in the extreme: on the south side a long line of perpendicular cliffs commences, which exposes a section of the geological nature of the country. The strata are of sandstone, and one layer was remarkable from being composed of a firmly-cemented conglomerate of pumice pebbles, which must have travelled more than four hundred miles, from the Andes.

The settlement is situated 18 miles up the river. On the way we passed the ruins of some fine "estancias," which a few years since had been destroyed by the Indians.

(...)The town is indifferently called El Carmen or Patagones. It is built on the face of a cliff which fronts the river, and many of the houses are excavated even in the sandstone. The river is about two or three hundred yards wide, and is deep and rapid..

The number of inhabitants does not exceed a few hundreds. These Spanish colonies do not, like our British ones, carry within themselves the elements of growth. Many Indians of pure blood reside here: the tribe of the Cacique Lucanee constantly have their Toldos on the outskirts of the town. The local government supplies them with provisions, by giving them all the old worn-out horses. These Indians are considered civilized; but what their character may have gained by a lesser degree of ferocity, is almost counter-balanced by their entire immorality. Some of the younger men are, however, improving."

Almost nobody calls it El Carmen any more. Its present name is more formal: Carmen de Patagones or simply Patagones. This city, which had its first school to the south of the Colorado River in 1821, is not the last populated place anymore and even has a more populated neighbourhood across the river: Viedma. Unfortunately, natives cannot be found any longer, but there are many young people willing to thrive. Tradition, nevertheless, remains intact.

A long horseback ride on wild territories

"To the northward of the Rio Negro, between it and the inhabited country near Buenos Ayres, the Spaniards have only one small settlement, recently established at Bahía Blanca. The distance in a straight line to Buenos Ayres is very nearly five hundred British miles. The wandering tribes of horse Indians, which have always occupied the greater part of this country, having of late much harassed the outlying estancias, the government at Buenos Ayres equipped some time since an army under the command of General Rosas for the purpose of exterminating them. The troops were now encamped on the banks of the Colorado; a river lying about eighty miles northward of the Río Negro. When General Rosas left Buenos Ayres he struck in a direct line across the unexplored plains: and as the country was thus pretty well cleared of Indians, he left behind him, at wide intervals, a small party of soldiers with a troop of horses (a posta), so as to be enabled to keep up a communication with the capital. As the Beagle intended to call at Bahía Blanca, I determined to proceed there by land; and ultimately I extended my plan to travel the whole way by the postas to Buenos Ayres."

August 11th

Mr. Harris, an Englishman residing at Patagones, a guide, and five Gauchos who were proceeding to the army on business, were my companions on the journey. The Colorado, as I have already said, is nearly eighty miles distant: and as we travelled slowly, we were two days and a half on the road. The whole line of country deserves scarcely a better name than that of a desert. (...) We halted for the night: at this instant an unfortunate cow was spied by the lynx-eyed Gauchos, who set off in full chace, and in a few minutes dragged her in with their lazos, and slaughtered her. We here had the four necessaries of life "en el campo,"–pasture for the horses, water (only a muddy puddle), meat and firewood.

This was the first night which I passed under the open sky, with the gear of the recado for my bed. There is high enjoyment in the independence of the Gaucho life –to be able at any moment to pull up your horse, and say, "Here we will pass the night." The death-like stillness of the plain, the dogs keeping watch, the gipsy-group of Gauchos making their beds round the fire, have left in my mind a strongly-marked picture of this first night, which will never be forgotten."

Darwin's poetic phrase on the independence of the "gauchos" has been limited in its action since the introduction of the wire fence more than 150 years ago. Domingo F. Sarmiento said in 1876: *"Prior to the wire fence, the whole country was a road"*.

Charles Darwin and Juan Manuel de Rosas

August 14th, 1833

"(...) The Colorado, at the pass where we crossed it, is only about sixty yards wide; generally it must be nearly double that width. Its course is very tortuous.

We were delayed crossing in the canoe by some immense troops of mares, which were swimming the river in order to follow a division of troops into the interior. A more ludicrous spectacle I never beheld than the hundreds and hundreds of heads, all directed one way, with pointed ears and distended snorting nostrils, appearing just above the water like a great shoal of some amphibious animal. Mare's flesh is the only food which the soldiers have when on an expedition. This gives them a great facility of movement; for the distance to which horses can be driven over these plains is quite surprising: I have been assured that an unloaded horse can travel a hundred miles a day for many days successively.

The encampment of General Rosas was close to the river. It consisted of a square formed by waggons, artillery, straw huts, etc. The soldiers were nearly all cavalry; and I should think such a villanous, banditti-like army was never before collected together. The greater number of men were of a mixed breed, between Negro, Indian, and Spaniard. I know not the reason, but men of such origin seldom have a good expression of countenance. (...)

We stayed two days at the Colorado.

My chief amusement was watching the Indian families.

It was supposed that General Rosas had about six hundred Indian allies.

Among the young women or chinas, some deserve to be called even beautiful. Their hair was coarse, but bright and black; and they wore it in two plaits hanging down to the waist.

Their ankles, and sometimes their waists, were ornamented by broad bracelets of blue beads. They ride like men, but with their knees tucked up much higher. Several of the men and women had their faces painted red, but I never saw the horizontal bands which are so common among the Fuegians. Their chief pride consists in having everything made of silver; I have seen a cacique with his spurs, stirrups, handle of his knife, and bridle made of this metal."

This is the famous Médano Redondo (Round Sand Dune), the exact place where Rosas' camp was situated. It is about fifteen kilometers away from the Mercedes Fort (Fortín Mercedes). The first noticeable change is that the Colorado River no longer crosses this place. Over a century ago, a huge flooding altered its course some three thousand meters northwards. The second alteration relates to the ownership of these lands. They have belonged to the Yunis family for many generations. Alberto (photograph) is his present proprietor. Some traces from Rosas' camp such as glass, metals or crockery can still be found. This almost forgotten spot witnessed the encounter of two great personalities: Charles Darwin and Juan Manuel de Rosas.

"General Rosas intimated a wish to see me; a circumstance which I was afterwards very glad of. He is a man of an extraordinary character, and has a most predominant influence in the country, which it seems probable he will use to its prosperity and advancement.* He is said to be the owner of seventy-four square leagues of land, and to have about three hundred thousand head of cattle. His estates are admirably managed, and are far more productive of corn than those of others. He first gained his celebrity by his laws for his own estancias, and by disciplining several hundred men, so as to resist with success the attacks of the Indians. (...)
In conversation he is enthusiastic, sensible, and very grave."

C.D.

Charles Darwin wrote these words in the first edition of his travelling journals in 1839. The book was made up of three volumes —under Captain FitzRoy's direction— and reproduced every detail of the H.M.S. Beagle expedition. A fourth volume would refer to statistics. Books were sold separately and were published by Henry Colburn. Volume III written by Darwin was rapidly sold out. In 1845 a new edition corrected by the author appeared.

* To the paragraph previously quoted, the Naturalist added this note: *"**This prophecy has turned out into a complete and pitiful mistake**".*

Watercolour on Charles Darwin painted by George Richmond in 1840.

Juan Manuel de Rosas drawn by Juan Alais on the same year he met Darwin: 1833.

Between Colorado River and Bahía Blanca

August 16th, 1833

"Having ridden about twenty-five miles, we came to a broad belt of sand dunes (…) Having crossed the sandy tract, we arrived in the evening at one of the post-houses; and, as the fresh horses were grazing at a distance, we determined to pass the night there.

The house was situated at the base of a ridge, between one and two hundred feet high –a most remarkable feature in this country. This posta was commanded by a negro lieutenant, born in Africa: to his credit be it said, there was not a rancho between the Colorado and Buenos Ayres in nearly such neat order as his.(…) I did not anywhere meet a more civil and obliging man than this negro; it was therefore the more painful to see that he would not sit down and eat with us. In the morning we sent for the horses very early, and started for another exhilarating gallop. We passed the Cabeza del Buey."

"Bahía Blanca scarcely deserves the name of a village. A few houses and the barracks for the troops are enclosed by a deep ditch and fortified wall. The settlement is only of recent standing (since 1828); and its growth has been one of trouble. The government of Buenos Ayres unjustly occupied it by force, instead of following the wise example of the Spanish Viceroys, who purchased the land near the older settlement of the Río Negro, from the Indians. Hence the need of the fortifications; hence the few houses and little cultivated land without the limits of the walls: even the cattle are not safe from the attacks of the Indians beyond the boundaries of the plain, on which the fortress stands.

The part of the harbour where the Beagle intended to anchor being distant twenty-five miles, I obtained from the Commandant a guide and horses, to take me to see whether she had arrived. Leaving the plain of green turf, which extended along the course of a little brook, we soon entered on a wide level waste consisting either of sand, saline marshes, or bare mud. Some parts were clothed by low thickets, and others with those succulent plants, which luxuriate only where salt abounds. Bad as the country was, ostriches, deers, agoutis, and armadilloes, were abundant. (...)

We found the Beagle had not arrived, and consequently set out on our return, but the horses soon tiring, we were obliged to bivouac on the plain. In the morning we had caught an armadillo, which, although a most excellent dish when roasted in its shell, did not make a very substantial breakfast and dinner for two hungry men."

Bahía Blanca has grown to the point of having the most important port in Argentina. Despite the loss in wildlife, the salt marshes Darwin crossed remain intact.

The origin of *On The Origin of Species?*

"We passed the night in Punta Alta, and I employed myself in searching for fossil bones; this point being a perfect catacomb for monsters of extinct races."

Charles Darwin

"The Beagle arrived here on the 24th of August, and a week afterwards sailed for the Plata. With Captain FitzRoy's consent I was left behind, to travel by land to Buenos Ayres."

While waiting in Bahia Blanca for the Beagle to arrive, Darwin and many crew members dedicated a lot of their time to digging clay terraces along the coastal front between Punta Alta and Pehuencó. He made significant and valuable discoveries.

In the following list he enumerates and declares:

"First, parts of three heads and other bones of the Megatherium, the huge dimensions of which are expressed by its name. Secondly, the Megalonyx, a great allied animal. Thirdly, the Scelidotherium, also an allied animal, of which I obtained a nearly perfect skeleton. It must have been as large as a rhinoceros: in the structure of its head it comes, according to Mr. Owen, nearest to the Cape Ant-eater, but in some other respects it approaches to the armadilloes. Fourthly, the Mylodon Darwinii, a closely related genus of little inferior size. Fifthly, another gigantic edental quadruped. Sixthly, a large animal, with an osseous coat in compartments, very like that of an armadillo. Seventhly, an extinct kind of horse, to which I shall have again to refer. Eighthly, a tooth of a Pachydermatous animal, probably the same with the Macrauchenia, a huge beast with a long neck like a camel, which I shall also refer to again. Lastly, the Toxodon, perhaps one of the strangest animals ever discovered: in size it equalled an elephant or megatherium, but the structure of its teeth. (...) Judging from the position of its eyes, ears, and nostrils, it was probably aquatic."

PART I.] No 1. [No. I. 8s.

THE

ZOOLOGY

OF

THE VOYAGE OF H.M.S. BEAGLE,

UNDER THE COMMAND OF CAPTAIN FITZROY,

DURING THE YEARS

1832 TO 1836.

PUBLISHED WITH THE APPROVAL OF THE LORDS COMMISSIONERS OF HER MAJESTY'S TREASURY.

Edited and Superintended by

CHARLES DARWIN, ESQ. M.A. F.G.S.

CORRESPONDING MEMBER OF THE ZOOLOGICAL SOCIETY, AND NATURALIST TO THE EXPEDITION.

FOSSIL MAMMALIA,

BY RICHARD OWEN, ESQ.

PROFESSOR OF ANATOMY AND PHYSIOLOGY IN THE ROYAL COLLEGE OF SURGEONS, LONDON.

LONDON:
SMITH, ELDER AND CO., 65, CORNHILL.
MDCCCXXXVIII.

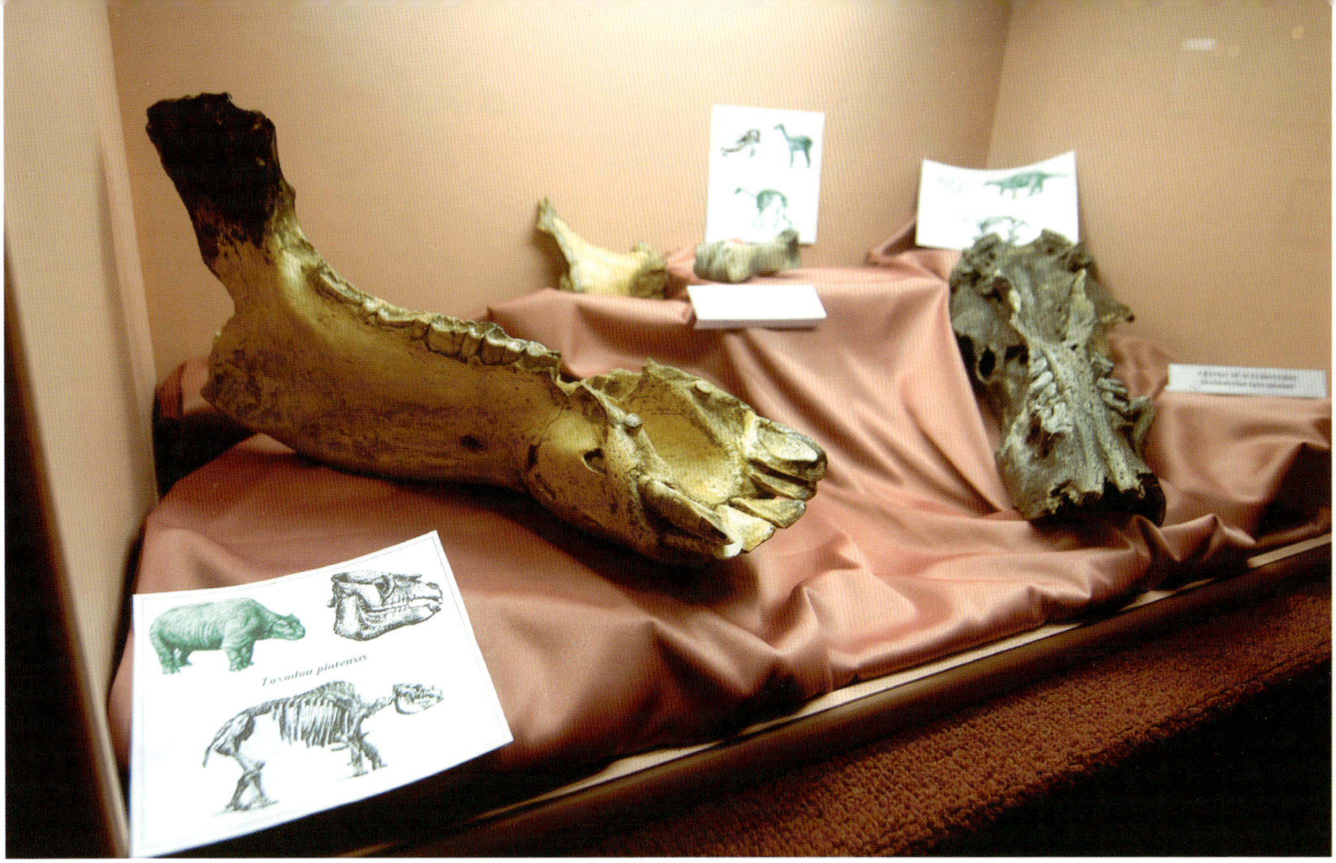

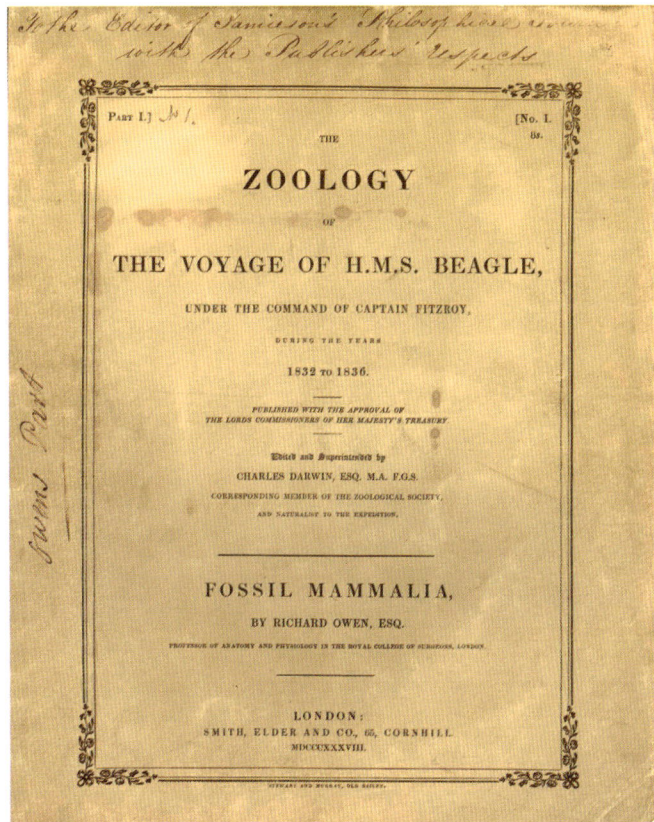

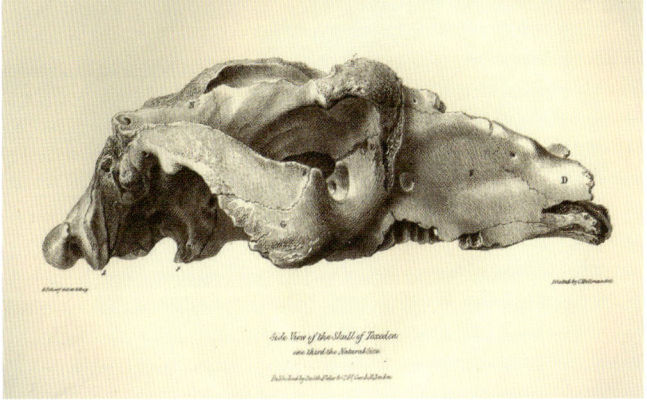

The famous toxodon: the drawn skull was part of the book Zoology of the H.M.S. Beagle by Richard Owen. The jaw is part of the permanent collection at the Charles Darwin Museum in Punta Alta. The following pages show the coast of Pehuencó, where the expedition members arrived in August 1833.

"South American ostrich" **

"I will now give an account of the habits of some of the more interesting birds which are common on the wild plains of Northern Patagonia; and first for the largest, or South American ostrich. The ordinary habits of the ostrich are familiar to every one. They live on vegetable matter, such as roots and grass; but at Bahia Blanca I have repeatedly seen three or four come down at low water to the extensive mud-banks which are then dry, for the sake, as the Gauchos say, of feeding on small fish. Although the ostrich in its habits is so shy, wary, and solitary, and although so fleet in its pace, it is caught without much difficulty by the Indian or Gaucho armed with the bolas. (...)

It is not generally known that ostriches readily take to the water. Mr. King informs me that at the Bay of San Blas, and at Port Valdés in Patagonia, he saw these birds swimming several times from island to island.

When swimming, very little of their bodies appear above water; their necks are extended a little forward, and their progress is slow. On two occasions I saw some ostriches swimming across the Santa Cruz River.

The inhabitants of the country readily distinguish, even at a distance, the cock bird from the hen. The former is larger and darker-coloured, and has a bigger head. Hen at the Río Negro in Northern Patagonia, I repeatedly heard the Gauchos talking of a very rare bird which they called Avestruz Petise. They described it as being less than the common ostrich (which is there abundant), but with a very close general resemblance. They said its colour was dark and mottled, and that its legs were shorter, and feathered lower down than those of the common ostrich. It is more easily caught by the bolas than the other species.

When at Port Desire, in Patagonia (lat. 48°), Mr. Martens shot an ostrich; and I looked at it, forgetting at the moment, in the most unaccountable manner, the whole subject of the Petises, and thought it was a not full-grown bird of the common sort. It was cooked and eaten before my memory returned.

Fortunately the head, neck, legs, wings, many of the larger feathers, and a large part of the skin, had been preserved; and from these a very nearly perfect specimen has been put together, and is now exhibited in the museum of the Zoological Society. Mr. Gould, in describing this new species, has done me the honour of calling it after my name.

Editor's note: Rhea Darwinii

C.D.

** Rhea Americana

On the way to Buenos Aires

"During my stay at Bahía Blanca, while waiting for the Beagle, the place was in a constant state of excitement, from rumours of wars and victories, between the troops of Rosas and the wild Indians. One day an account came that a small party forming one of the postas on the line to Buenos Ayres, had been found all murdered."

I transcribe these lines to reinforce the image of the scenery awaiting Darwin in his long ride to Buenos Aires. His courage to face such trials triggered this project. It is not the purpose of this edition to go into details, but these are rich in historical descriptions, especially during the war against the Indians. I encourage you to read his travel journal in depth, especially the one published by Editorial Elefante Blanco, for its truthfulness towards the original version. In order to fully understand this special moment in our history, the book "Rosas, aportes para su historia"*, by Roberto Celesia (Ediciones Peuser), is a magnificent complement that records and describes those bloody years.*

September 8th

"I hired a Gaucho to accompany me on my ride to Buenos Ayres, though with some difficulty, as the father of one man was afraid to let him go, and another, who seemed willing, was described to me as so fearful, that I was afraid to take him, for I was told that even if he saw an ostrich at a distance, he would mistake it for an Indian, and would fly like the wind away. The distance to Buenos Ayres is about four hundred miles, and nearly the whole way through an uninhabited country. We started early in the morning; ascending a few hundred feet from the basin of green turf on which Bahía Blanca stands, we entered on a wide desolate plain. (...)

After a long gallop, having changed horses twice, we reached the Río Sauce: it is a deep, rapid, little stream, not above twenty-five feet wide. The second posta on the road to Buenos Ayres stands on its banks; a little above there is a ford for horses, where the water does not reach to the horses' belly; but from that point, in its course to the sea, it is quite impassable, and hence makes a most useful barrier against the Indians.

As it was early in the afternoon when we arrived, we took fresh horses, and a soldier for a guide, and started for the Sierra de la Ventana. This mountain is visible from the anchorage at Bahía Blanca; and Captain FitzRoy calculates its height to be 3.340 feet —an altitude very remarkable on this eastern side of the continent. I am not aware that any foreigner, previous to my visit, had ascended this mountain; and indeed very few of the soldiers at Bahía Blanca knew anything about it. Hence we heard of beds of coal, of gold and silver, of caves, and of forests, all of which inflamed my curiosity, only to disappoint it.

(...) I do not think Nature ever made a more solitary, desolate pile of rock."

September 10th

"In the morning, having fairly scudded before the gale, we arrived by the middle of the day at the Sauce posta. On the road we saw great numbers of deer, and near the mountain a guanaco."

```
Captain FitzRoy made excellent calculations, for the
average height of the mountain mass of Ventana is
approximately of one thousand meters. The highest
summit is the Cerro Tres Picos, with 1.239 meters.
The deers described by Darwin were those from las
Pampas, which are today considered endangered
species. According to a specialist, Doctor Alfredo
Balcarce, only some 300 animals remain. The red deer
-introduced over one hundred years ago- has
massively replaced the Pampas deer.
```

September 11th

"Proceeded to the third posta.
The road was uninteresting, over a dry grassy plain.
Soon afterwards we perceived by the cloud of dust, that a party of horsemen were coming towards us. They turned out to be a party of Bernantio's friendly tribe, going to a salina for salt. The Indians gave us good-humoured nods as they passed at full gallop, driving before them a troop of horses, and followed by a train of lanky dogs."

September 12th and 13th

"I stayed at this posta two days, waiting for a troop of soldiers, which General Rosas had the kindness to send to inform me, would shortly travel to Buenos Ayres; and he advised me to take the opportunity of the escort. (...) After dinner the soldiers divided themselves into two parties for a trial of skill with the bolas."

September 14th

"As the soldiers belonging to the next posta meant to return, and we should together make a party of five, and all armed, I determined not to wait for the expected troops. (...)
After galloping some leagues, we came to a low swampy country, which extends for nearly eighty miles northward, as far as the Sierra Tapalguen.
At night we had some difficulty in finding, amidst the swamps, a dry place for our bivouac."

September 15th

"Rose very early in the morning, and shortly after passed the posta where the Indians had murdered the five soldiers. The officer had eighteen chuzo wounds in his body. By the middle of the day, after a hard gallop, we reached the fifth posta: on account of some difficulty in procuring horses we stayed there the night. As this point was the most exposed on the whole line, twenty-one soldiers were stationed here; at sunset they returned from hunting, bringing with them seven deer, three ostriches, and many armadilloes and partridges."

Route 3 could be considered the perfect evolution
of the old line of posts Darwin travelled between
Bahía Blanca and Buenos Aires.

"We did not reach the posta on the Río Tapalguen till after it was dark. At supper, from something which was said, I was suddenly struck with horror at thinking that I was eating one of the favourite dishes of the country, namely, a half-formed calf, long before its proper time of birth. It turned out to be Puma; the meat is very white, and remarkably like veal in taste"

September 17th

"We followed the course of the Río Tapalguen, through a very fertile country, to the ninth posta. Tapalguen itself, or the town of Tapalguen, if it may be so called, consists of a perfectly level plain, studded over, as far as the eye can reach, with the toldos, or oven-shaped huts of the Indians. The families of the friendly Indians, who were fighting on the side of Rosas, resided here. We met and passed many young Indian women.

They, as well as many of the young men, were strikingly handsome,–their fine ruddy complexions being the picture of health."

The course Charles Darwin followed along the Tapalqué stream led him through the park of Jorge Lounge's ranch, La Isolina. His forefathers arrived in the area in 1854, in the midst of the war against the Indians. Due to their valour and the good relationship they established with the natives, they gained acres which multiplied throughout the years. In 1899 they bought these lands and in 1920 they built the main house. Besides agriculture and stockbreeding, they devote themselves to the area of tourism and are highly recognized for their excellent services.

September 18th

We had a very long ride this day. At the twelfth posta, which is seven leagues south of the Rio Salado, we came to the first estancia with cattle and white women. Afterwards we had to ride for many miles through a country flooded with water above our horses' knees. (...)

It was nearly dark when we arrived at the Salado; the stream was deep, and about forty yards wide; we slept at one of the great estancias of General Rosas. It was fortified, and of such an extent, that arriving in the dark I thought it was a town and fortress. In the morning we saw immense herds of cattle, the general here having seventy-four square leagues of land."

For decades, the bridge on the Salado River, on route 3, has prevented many travelers from getting wet. Obviously farms with such large extensions as Rosas´cannot be found any longer.

Charles Darwin in Buenos Aires

September 20th

"We arrived by the middle of the day at Buenos Ayres. The outskirts of the city looked quite pretty, with the agave hedges, and groves of olive, peach, and willow trees, all just throwing out their fresh green leaves. I rode to the house of Mr. Lumb, an English merchant, to whose kindness and hospitality during my stay in the country, I was greatly indebted.

The city of Buenos Ayres is large;* and I should think one of the most regular in the world. Every street is at right angles to the one it crosses, and the parallel ones being equidistant, the houses are collected into solid squares of equal dimensions, which are called quadras. On the other hand, the houses themselves are hollow squares; all the rooms opening into a neat little courtyard. They are generally only one story high, with flat roofs, which are fitted with seats, and are much frequented by the inhabitants in summer. In the centre of the town is the Plaza, where the public offices, fortress, cathedral, &c., stand. Here also, the old viceroys, before the revolution, had their palaces. The general assemblage of buildings possesses considerable architectural beauty, although none individually can boast of any."

*Charles Darwin stayed on 56 de la Paz Street (known today as Reconquista), at Mr Lumb's house. Edward Lumb was a fellow countryman who not only sent some fossils he found in his expeditions to England, but also became a useful contact with whom Darwin exchanged letters many times. For example, the time when he retold his frustrated visit on board the Beagle, on August, 2nd, 1832, when they couldn't disembark. This was the third time Darwin arrived in Buenos Aires, a city that had caused a good impression on him. This is what he wrote on the journal he used during his second visit:

6th [November 1832] Very busy in collecting informations & specimens Shopping & ladies

This new stay in the city (from Friday 20th, September to Thursday, 26th) had a new positive impression on him. A couple of months later, in Uruguay, he stated amongst some friends that women in Buenos Aires were the most beautiful in the world, and that no one wore hair combs as big as they did.

His fourth and last visit wouldn't be as pleasing, since he would find a city taken by General Balcarce's followers and Rosas' supporters.

Original Lithograph BN de Aust v. FW. Kahler-Hamburg-courtesy of Fundación YPF

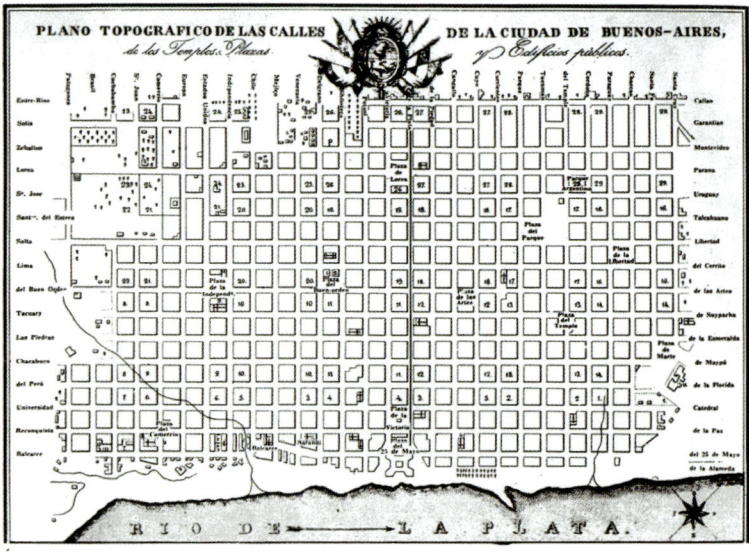

Charles Darwin visited Buenos Aires, a city with a population of 60 thousand inhabitants. Today, it is a city of three million souls and ten million people need to be added if its outskirts are taken into account. Some places have remained unaltered since the naturalist's visit. Plaza de Mayo is one of them. In contrast, Puerto Madero (previous double page) or Catalinas Norte, in the neighbourhood of Retiro, are clear examples of urban evolution.

from Buenos Aires to Santa Fé

September 27th

"In the evening I set out on an excursion to Santa Fé, which is situated nearly three hundred English miles from Buenos Ayres, on the banks of the Paraná. The roads in the neighbourhood of the city, after the rainy weather, were extraordinarily bad. I should never have thought it possible for a bullock waggon to have crawled along: as it was, they scarcely went at the rate of a mile an hour. (...)

We passed a train of waggons and a troop of beasts on their road to Mendoza. The distance is about 580 geographical miles, and the journey is generally performed in fifty days. These waggons are very long, narrow, and thatched with reeds; they have only two wheels, the diameter of which in some cases is as much as ten feet. Each is drawn by six bullocks."

September 28th

"We passed the small town of Luxan, where there is a wooden bridge over the river —a most unusual convenience in this country. We passed also Areco. The plains appeared level, but were not so in fact; for in various places the horizon was distant. The estancias are here wide apart; for there is little good pasture, owing to the land being covered by beds either of an acrid clover. (...) In some parts they were as high as the horse's back.

Upon asking at a house whether robbers were numerous, I was answered, "The thistles are not up yet!"

Roads have improved and thistles, high enough to cover a horse, are no longer visible. Unfortunately, thieves or "pirates of the asphalt" are still very active.

The "small city" changed. Worshippers of the Virgin of Luján turned the town into a pilgrimage destination. Its centennial cathedral (which started to be built in 1890) is one of the most important churches in America.

29th and 30th

"We continued to ride over plains of the same character. At San Nicolás I first saw the noble river of the Paraná. At the foot of the cliff on which the town stands, some large vessels were at anchor."

Before arriving at Rosario, we crossed the Saladillo, a stream of fine clear running water, but too saline to drink. Rosario is a large town built on a dead level plain, which forms a cliff about sixty feet high over the Parana. The river here is very broad, with many islands, which are low and wooded, as is also the opposite shore. The view would resemble that of a great lake, if it were not for the linearshaped islets, which alone give the idea of running water.

The real grandeur, however, of an immense river like this, is derived from reflecting how important a means of communication and commerce it forms between one nation and another; to what a distance it travels; and from how vast a territory it drains the great body of fresh water which flows past your feet."

C.D.

Charles Darwin and José de San Martín

In the vicinity of Rosario, Charles Darwin states that in the morning of October 1st, 1833, they departed very early and that on the coast of Tercero River (today known as Carcarañá) he spent most of the day in search for fossils with excellent results. Where did he depart from? Where did he spend the night? His records indicate that he slept at San Carlos' School, which was located in the Convent of San Lorenzo, the same that witnessed the triumph of General José de San Martín against the Spaniards (February 3rd, 1813). The English youngster and the courageous general walked the same corridors with only twenty years of difference. Later on we will see that San Lorenzo was not the only place of coincidence between them. Founded in 1810, the school celebrated two centuries of uninterrupted Franciscan education. In its first years he only occupied a room in the convent, but due to the increasing number of pupils he ordered the construction of his own building behind the Franciscan walls.

More than two hundred years come together in these pictures: the future, held by the hand of promising students, and the historical past, represented by the corridors Darwin walked towards his room and the belfry San Martín climbed to spy on Spanish ships on the slope of the Paraná River.

October 2nd

We passed through Corunda, which, from the luxuriance of its gardens, was one of the prettiest villages I saw.

From this point to Santa Fé the road is not very safe. The western side of the Paraná northward, ceases to be inhabited; and hence the Indians sometimes comedown thus far, and waylay travellers. (...)

We passed some houses that had been ransacked and since deserted; we saw also a spectacle, which my guides viewed with high satisfaction; it was the skeleton of an Indian with the dried skin hanging on the bones, suspended to the branch of a tree."

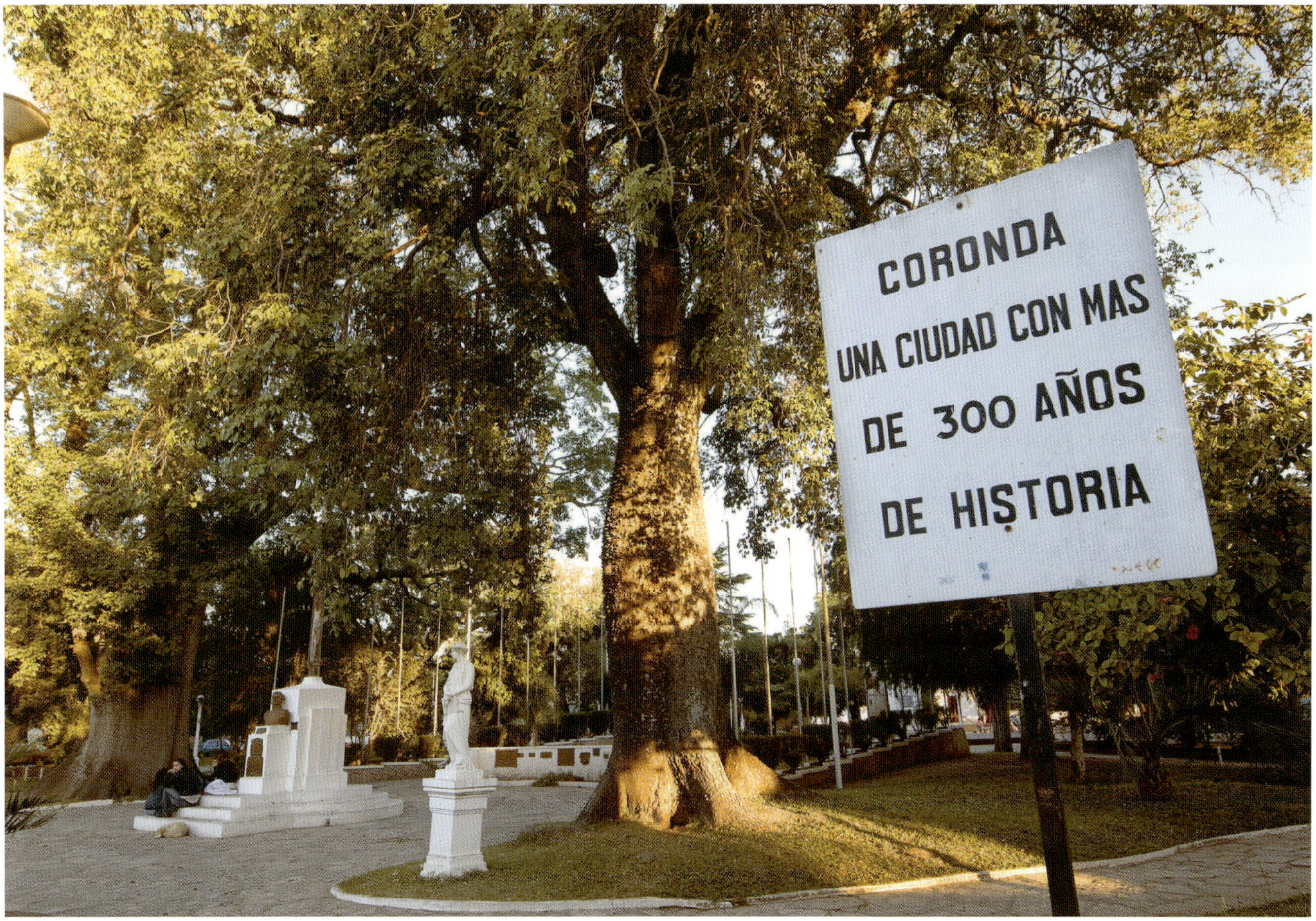
CORONDA
UNA CIUDAD CON MAS
DE 300 AÑOS
DE HISTORIA

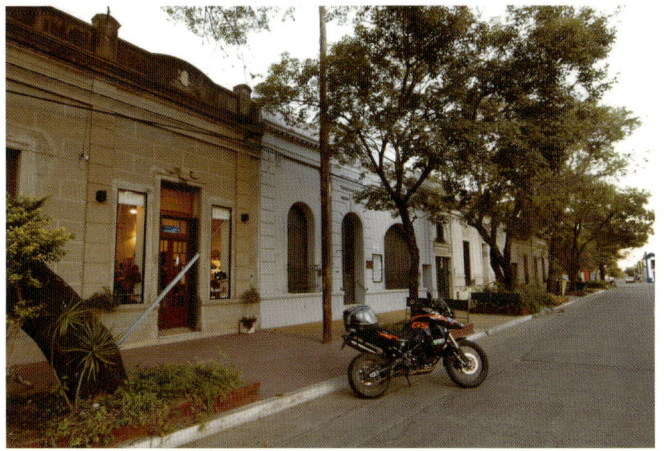

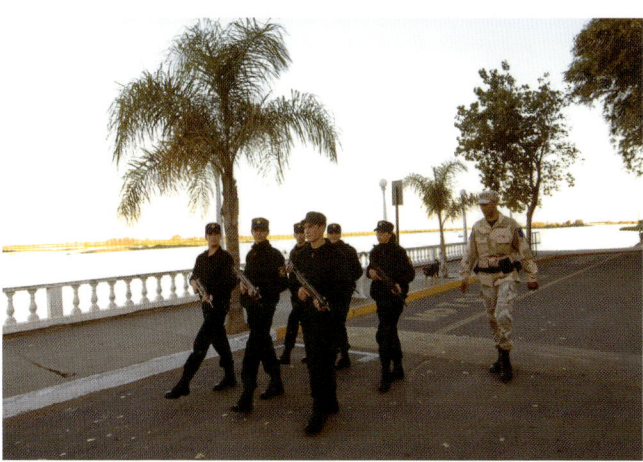

Santa Fé City

October 3rd and 4th

"I was confined for these two days to my bed by a headache. A good-natured old woman, who attended me, wished me to try many odd remedies. A common practice is, to bind an orange-leaf or a bit of black plaster to each temple: and a still more general plan is, to split a bean into halves, moisten them, and place one on each temple, where they will easily adhere. (...)

Santa Fé is a quiet little town, and is kept clean and in good order. The governor, Lopez, was a common soldier at the time of the revolution; but has now been seventeen years in power.

This stability of government is owing to his tyrannical habits; for tyranny seems as yet better adapted to these countries than republicanism. The governor's favourite occupation is hunting Indians: a short time since he slaughtered forty-eight, and sold the children at the rate of three or four pounds apiece."

October 5th

"We crossed the Paraná to Santa Fé Bajada, a town on the opposite shore. The passage took some hours, as the river here consisted of a labyrinth of small streams, separated by low wooded islands."

C.D.

Entre Ríos yesterday

October 5th

"The Bajada is the capital of Entre Ríos. In 1825 the town contained 6.000 inhabitants, and the province 30.000; yet, few as the inhabitants are, no province has suffered more from bloody and desperate revolutions. They boast here of representatives, ministers, a standing army, and governors: so it is no wonder that they have their revolutions. At some future day this must be one of the richest countries of La Plata. The soil is varied and productive; and its almost insular form gives it two grand lines of communication by the rivers Paraná and Uruguay.

I was delayed here five days, and employed myself in examining the geology of the surrounding country, which was very interesting. We here see at the bottom of the cliffs, beds containing sharks' teeth and sea-shells of extinct species, passing above into an indurated marl (...)

In the Pampaean deposit at the Bajada I found the osseous armour of a gigantic armadillo-like animal, the inside of which, when the earth was removed, was like a great cauldron."

Darwin's experience in unburying a glyptodont on the Paraná riverside must have been similar to Mario Vigniolo's, aged twelve, who found similar traces on a gully by the Perico Flaco stream, seven kilometers away from Villa Darwin, Uruguay, and 280 kilometers from the city of Paraná, Entre Ríos.
Mario himself took these pictures with a laptop. These photographs represent an invaluable paleontological document. These fossils can be found in the Alejandro Berro Museum, in Mercedes.

GENTILEZA JORGE BARLETTA

Entre Ríos today

It is interesting to analyze, in this case, some numbers on the province of Entre Ríos, with regard to Darwin's words two centuries ago.

Its population changed significantly. Today Paraná (in Darwin's times known as Santa Fé Bajada) has 270 thousand inhabitants, from a total of 1.300.000 people in the whole province. The area is still in the process of fulfilling the prophecy of becoming one of the richest provinces of the Plata basin. Entre Ríos contributes to the 2.6% of the national GDP, occupying the sixth place. The GDP per person is lower than the general average in Argentina: about USD5.600, against USD 8.600 at a national level.

Its wealth comes from agriculture and livestock. Entre Ríos is the main rice and citrus fruit- producing/exporting province. It has 1.300.000 livestock distributed in 21 thousand establishments (50 hectares or more each).

Dodging jaguars in the Paraná River

October 12th

"I had intended to push my excursion further, but not being quite well, I was compelled to return by a balandra, or one-masted vessel of about a hundred tons' burden, which was bound to Buenos Ayres. As the weather was not fair, we moored early in the day to a branch of a tree on one of the islands. The Paraná is full of islands, which undergo a constant round of decay and renovation (…)

They all present one character; numerous willows and a few other trees are bound together by a great variety of creeping plants, thus forming a thick jungle. These thickets afford a retreat for capybaras and jaguars. The fear of the latter animal quite destroyed all pleasure in scrambling through the woods. This evening I had not proceeded a hundred yards, before finding indubitable signs of the recent presence of the tiger, I was obliged to come back. On every island there were tracks; and as on the former excursion 'el rastro de los Indios' had been the subject of conversation, so in this was 'el rastro del tigre'."

The yaguareté (jaguar) has become extinct in this area for many years now. The few remaining have lost 85 per cent of their natural territory. According to the organization Red Yaguareté barely 250 animals exist in a limited geographical radius. For more info visit http://www.redyaguarete.org.ar

"The wooded banks of the great rivers appear to be the favourite haunts of the jaguar; but south of the Plata, I was told that they frequented the reeds bordering lakes: wherever they are, they seem to require water. Their common prey is the capybara, so that it is generally said, where capybaras are numerous there is little danger from the jaguar.

On the Paraná they have killed many wood-cutters, and have even entered vessels at night. There is a man now living in the Bajada, who, coming up from below when it was dark, was seized on the deck; he escaped, however, with the loss of the use of one arm. When the floods drive these animals from the islands, they are most dangerous. I was told that a few years since a very large one found its way into a church at Santa Fé: two padres entering one after the other were killed, and a third, who came to see what was the matter, escaped with difficulty. The beast was destroyed by being shot from a corner of the building which was unroofed. (…)

The jaguar is killed, without much difficulty, by the aid of dogs baying and driving him up a tree, where he is despatched with bullets."

C.D.

And now... Tigre

October 20th

"Being arrived at the mouth of the Paraná, and as I was very anxious to reach Buenos Ayres, I went on shore at Las Conchas, with the intention of riding there. Upon landing, I found to my great surprise that I was to a certain degree a prisoner. A violent revolution having broken out, all the ports were laid under an embargo. I could not return to my vessel, and as for going by land to the city, it was out of the question. After a long conversation with the commandant, I obtained permission to go the next day to General Rolor, who commanded a division of the rebels on this side the capital. In the morning I rode to the encampment. The general, officers, and soldiers, all appeared, and I believe really were, great villains. (...)

General "Rolor", as Charles writes in his diary, wasn't other than Mariano Benito Rolón (1790-1849), who, when the restorers´ revolution broke out on October, 11th 1833, took sides with the revolutionaries and laid siege to Buenos Aires for several days. General Rolón did it from Las Conchas (today known as Tigre) whereas General Pinedo directed it from Quilmes, the opposite side.

"The general told me that the city was in a state of close blockade, and that all he could do was to give me a passport to the commander-in-chief of the rebels at Quilmes. We had therefore to take a great sweep round the city, and it was with much difficulty that we procured horses. My reception at the encampment was quite civil, but I was told it was impossible that I could be allowed to enter the city. I was very anxious about this, as I anticipated the Beagle's departure from the Río de la Plata earlier than it took place. Having mentioned, however, General Rosas's obliging kindness to me when at the Colorado, magic itself could not have altered circumstances quicker than did this conversation. I was instantly told that though they could not give me a passport, if I chose to leave my guide and horses, I might pass their sentinels. I was too glad to accept of this, and an officer was sent with me to give directions that I should not be stopped at the bridge."

Charles Darwin was a privileged witness and he interviewed the revolution's main protagonists. The events came to an end on November 4th, 1833 with Governor Juan Ramón Balcarce´s resignation. A few days later, Generals Pinedo and Rolón entered the city as commanders of six thousand horsemen and one thousand infantrymen. General Viamonte took power but didn´t last long. In 1835 Juan Manuel de Rosas became Governor again with full faculties and the sum of all powers.

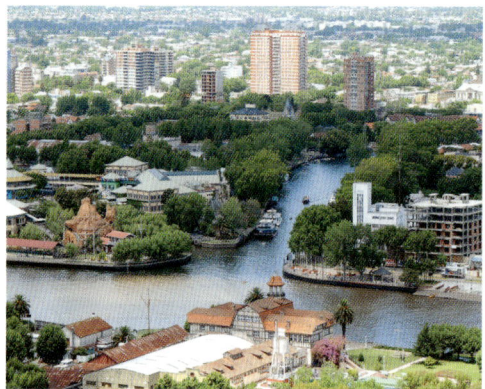

The area of Tigre is today one of the most important places in the province of Buenos Aires. With an extensive insular zone, its economy is varied and ranges from big industries to small agricultural exploitations on the islands. Tourism is a vital resource.

Back in Uruguay
Touring Colonia del Sacramento

Darwin's fears on the departure of the H.M.S. Beagle from the River de la Plata towards South were unfounded. After being forced to stay fifteen days in Buenos Aires, he managed to cross to Montevideo (on a long and annoying journey, according to his description), only to find out that FitzRoy had no intention of setting sail yet. Consequently, he rapidly headed for a new tour throughout Uruguay.

November 14th

"We left Monte Video in the afternoon. I intended to proceed to Colonia del Sacramento, situated on the northern bank of the Plata and opposite to Buenos Ayres, and thence, following up the Uruguay, to the village of Mercedes on the Río Negro (one of the many rivers of this name in South America), and from this point to return direct to Monte Video."

November 17th

"We arrived at mid-day at Colonia del Sacramento. (…) The town is built on a stony promontory something in the same manner as at Monte Video. It is strongly fortified, but both fortifications and town suffered much in the Brazilian war. It is very ancient; and the irregularity of the streets, and the surrounding groves of old orange and peach trees, gave it a pretty appearance. The church is a curious ruin; it was used as a powder-magazine, and was struck by lightning in one of the ten thousand thunder-storms of the Río Plata. Two-thirds of the building were blown away to the very foundation; and the rest stands a shattered and curious monument of the united powers of lightning and gunpowder."

The old quarters of Colonia, with its 1857 lighthouse is one of the main places for tourism in the city. Preserving its architecture is a commitment that has been made by the different governments for many years.

Charles Darwin in Carmelo & Punta Gorda

November 19th

"Passing the valley of Las Vacas, we slept at a house of a North American, who worked a lime-kiln on the Arroyo de las Víboras. In the morning we rode to a projecting headland on the banks of the river, called Punta Gorda. On the way we tried to find a jaguar. There were plenty of fresh tracks, and we visited the trees, on which they are said to sharpen their claws; but we did not succeed in disturbing one. From this point the Río Uruguay presented to our view a noble volume of water. From the clearness and rapidity of the stream, its appearance was far superior to that of its neighbour the Paraná. On the opposite coast, several branches from the latter river entered the Uruguay. As the sun was shining, the two colours of the waters could be seen quite distinct.

In the evening we proceeded on our road towards Mercedes on the Río Negro."

This mention in his travelling journal is briefer and less technical than other entries during his trip. In successive brown-leathered notebooks (of 15, 5 by 10 centimeters) Darwin kept record of key words, names, loose phrases, and a great deal of technical data. Much of this information had to do with his outstanding education as a geologist. His original writings on the day of his arrival at Carmelo started like this:

(19th) [November 1833] WNW of Sierra de St Juan Mortar – Hills appear to run N & S between the head of two streams. – Calera de los Huérfanos 4 Leagues before arriving at Las Vacas Mortar formation. (V Specimen) Generally more white & pure: a few more hundred yards further on – a highly ferruginous sandstone with specks of quartz mingled irregularly with a paler & less sandy sort –This occurs irregularly till their are some low hills near Las Vacas – Here the same rock occurs very abundantly. –& in section of "A tres Bocas" is seen lying over pale Tosca abounding with calcareous matter & concretion – The summit of the hill granite – in this manner there were repeated alternations of gneiss granite & this Sandstone. – The latter here contained large fragments of Quartz. –Wood Much wood like Corinda. – Las Vacas straggling thatched town wit on Riacho with many small vessels: much delay & trouble. – No Biscatcha. Cuervos soar in flock: –

```
Historical places: the first bridge of Uruguay
and the first kilometer of la Plata River.
The sign in Médanos de Punta Gorda farm club
says: "Darwin has been here."
```

The notebook Charles used in Punta Gorda reveals juicy information:

House 108 years old. – old woman of 90 years old positively states that very early in her life no trees ?! no trees except one orange tree Lime (...) Curious subterranean arch at Colonia. – 3.500 small green parrots killed in one field of corn near Colonia. – Jaguar (went out hunting) cut trees on each side with claws sharpening plagued by Foxes barking never return to dead body: Gato pájaro1 inhabits Banda Oriental.

As mentioned in previous pages, jaguars can't be found on these riversides any longer, but there is a rich fauna that includes all types of birds, and some wild cats like the bobcat. The beach on the Uruguay River is a good place to spot them. With ongoing positive projects, as Casa Chic and Médanos de Punta Gorda, Darwin's spirit is intact.

On the way to Patagonia

December 6th

"The Beagle sailed from the Río Plata, never again to enter its muddy stream. Our course was directed to Port Desire, on the coast of Patagonia. Before proceeding any further, I will here put together a few observations made at sea.

Several times when the ship has been some miles off the mouth of the Plata, and at other times when off the shores of Northern Patagonia, we have been surrounded by insects. One evening, when we were about ten miles from the Bay of San Blas, vast numbers of butterflies, in bands or flocks of countless myriads, extended as far as the eye could range. Even by the aid of a telescope it was not possible to see a space free from butterflies. The seamen cried out "it was snowing butterflies," and such in fact was the appearance. (...) On another occasion, when seventeen miles off Cape Corrientes, I had a net overboard to catch pelagic animals. Upon drawing it up, to my surprise I found a considerable number of beetles in it, and although in the open sea, they did not appear much injured by the salt water.

I thought that these insects had been blown from the shore; but upon reflecting that out of the eight species four were aquatic, and two others partly so in their habits, it appeared to me most probable that they were floated into the sea by a small stream which drains a lake near Cape Corrientes. (...)

On several occasions, when the Beagle has been within the mouth of the Plata, the rigging has been coated with the web of the Gossamer Spider.

The ship was sixty miles distant from the land, in the direction of a steady though light breeze. Vast numbers of a small spider, about one-tenth of an inch in length, and of a dusky red colour, were attached to the webs. There must have been, I should suppose, some thousands on the ship. (...)

While sailing a little south of the Plata on one very dark night, the sea presented a wonderful and most beautiful spectacle. There was a fresh breeze, and every part of the surface, which during the day is seen as foam, now glowed with a pale light. The vessel drove before her bows two billows of liquid phosphorus, and in her wake she was followed by a milky train."

C.D.

Any Sunday in the year 2010: many vessels sail the La Plata River.

H.M.S. Beagle in Port Desire

December 23rd

"We arrived at Port Desire, situated in latitude 47°, on the coast of Patagonia. The creek runs for about twenty miles inland, with an irregular width. The Beagle anchored a few miles within the entrance, in front of the ruins of an old Spanish settlement.

The same evening I went on shore. The first landing in any new country is very interesting, and especially when, as in this case, the whole aspect bears the stamp of a marked and individual character. At the height of between two and three hundred feet above some masses of porphyry a wide plain extends, which is truly characteristic of Patagonia. The surface is quite level, and is composed of well-rounded shingle mixed with a whitish earth. Here and there scattered tufts of brown wiry grass are supported, and, still more rarely, some low thorny bushes. The weather is dry and pleasant (...)."

C.D.

BRITANNIA OR TOWER ROCK, PORT DESIRE.

ANCHORAGE, AND SPANISH RUINS, PORT DESIRE.

UPPER PART OF PORT DESIRE INLET.

BIVOUAC AT THE HEAD OF PORT DESIRE INLET.

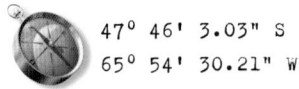
47° 46' 3.03" S
65° 54' 30.21" W

Brittania, Tower Rock... or The Toba Stone. This rock promontory remains exactly the same as Conrad Martens drew it two centuries ago. Visible from the dock of Port Desire, it is a living memory of past times.

Charles Darwin and a small crew were in command of Mr. Chaffers and they went upriver the Deseado stream for a few days. On his journal, the naturalist wrote: "I don't think I ever saw a more remote place in the world than this rocky crack in such extensive plain."

H.M.S. Beagle in Port San Julián

January 9th, 1834

"Before it was dark the Beagle anchored in the fine spacious harbour of Port St. Julian, situated about one hundred and ten miles to the south of Port Desire. We remained here eight days. The country is nearly similar to that of Port Desire, but perhaps rather more sterile. One day a party accompanied Captain Fitz Roy on a long walk round the head of the harbour. We were eleven hours without tasting any water, and some of the party were quite exhausted. From the summit of a hill (since well named Thirsty Hill) a fine lake was spied, and two of the party proceeded with concerted signals to show whether it was fresh water. What was our disappointment to find a snow-white expanse of salt, crystallized in great cubes!"

The geography surrounding San Julián Port does not vary much. The landscape is mysterious and devastating.

A few kilometers away from San Julián, lies the tomb of Lieutenant R. Sholl, a crew member from the previous H.M.S. Beagle mission on these coasts. The plaque in his honour has a mistake on it: it says he died in June 1828, and in fact his death was in January. Major Phillip Parker King, on board the Adventure, was commander in chief of the expedition. Everybody regretted the young lieutenant's death, as recorded in the ship's logbook.

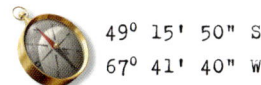
49° 15' 50" S
67° 41' 40" W

The geology of Patagonia is interesting. Differently from Europe, where the tertiary formations appear to have accumulated in bays, here along hundreds of miles of coast we have one great deposit, including many tertiary shells, all apparently extinct. The most common shell is a massive gigantic oyster, sometimes even a foot in diameter. These beds are covered by others of a peculiar soft white stone, including much gypsum, and resembling chalk, but really of a pumiceous nature. It is highly remarkable, from being composed, to at least one-tenth part of its bulk, of Infusoria: Professor Ehrenberg has already ascertained in it thirty oceanic forms. This bed extends for 500 miles along the coast, and probably for a considerably greater distance. At Port St. Julian its thickness is more than 800 feet!"

Cabo Curioso is a few kilometers away from Port San Julián. The fossilized oysters are still part of the Patagonian landscape.

"At Port San Julián, in some red mud capping the gravel on the 90-feet plain, I found half the skeleton of the Macrauchenia Patachonica, a remarkable quadruped, full as large as a camel. It belongs to the same division of the Pachydermata with the rhinoceros, tapir, and palæotherium; but in the structure of the bones of its long neck it shows a clear relation to the camel, or rather to the guanaco and llama." (...)

"It is impossible to reflect on the changed state of the American continent without the deepest astonishment. Formerly it must have swarmed with great monsters: now we find mere pigmies, compared with the antecedent, allied races"

Charles Darwin, Port San Julián, January 1834

Expedition to Santa Cruz River

April 13th, 1834

"The Beagle anchored within the mouth of the Santa Cruz. This river is situated about sixty miles south of Port San Julian. During the last voyage Captain Stokes proceeded thirty miles up it, but then, from the want of provisions, was obliged to return. Excepting what was discovered at that time, scarcely anything was known about this large river. Captain FitzRoy now determined to follow its course as far as time would allow. On the 18th three whale-boats started, carrying three weeks' provisions; and the party consisted of twenty-five souls —a force which would have been sufficient to have defied a host of Indians. With a strong flood-tide and a fine day we made a good run, soon drank some of the fresh water, and were at night nearly above the tidal influence.

The river here assumed a size and appearance which, even at the highest point we ultimately reached, was scarcely diminished. It was generally from three to four hundred yards broad, and in the middle about seventeen feet deep. The rapidity of the current, which in its whole course runs at the rate of from four to six knots an hour, is perhaps its most remarkable feature. The water is of a fine blue colour, but with a slight milky tinge, and not so transparent as at first sight would have been expected. It flows over a bed of pebbles, like those which compose the beach and the surrounding plains."

 50° 07. 55" S
68° 23. 41" W

Precisely 176 years later, also on April 13 th, I find myself in the same place the H.M.S. Beagle anchored to get some planks fixed and check on its keel. Captain FitzRoy took advantage of the tides to beach the boat some five hundred meters further from the place I had found the hermit penguin. The landscape is almost the same, but with an important evolution. Behind me (not seen in the photograph) is Punta Quilla (keel), a port in Santa Cruz which pays homage to the event I told you. The expedition departed from this place upriver.

April 19th

"Against so strong a current it was, of course, quite impossible to row or sail: consequently the three boats were fastened together head and stern, two hands left in each, and the rest came on shore to track. As the general arrangements made by Captain FitzRoy were very good for facilitating the work of all, and as all had a share in it, I will describe the system. The party, including every one, was divided into two spells, each of which hauled at the tracking line alternately for an hour and a half.

(...) During this day we tracked but a short distance, for there were many islets, covered by thorny bushes, and the channels between them were shallow."

```
Arriving at Luis Piedra Buena, the bridge on
Route 3 on the Santa Cruz River. In the same
area, the small islands Darwin mentions in his
journal, made navigation difficult.
```

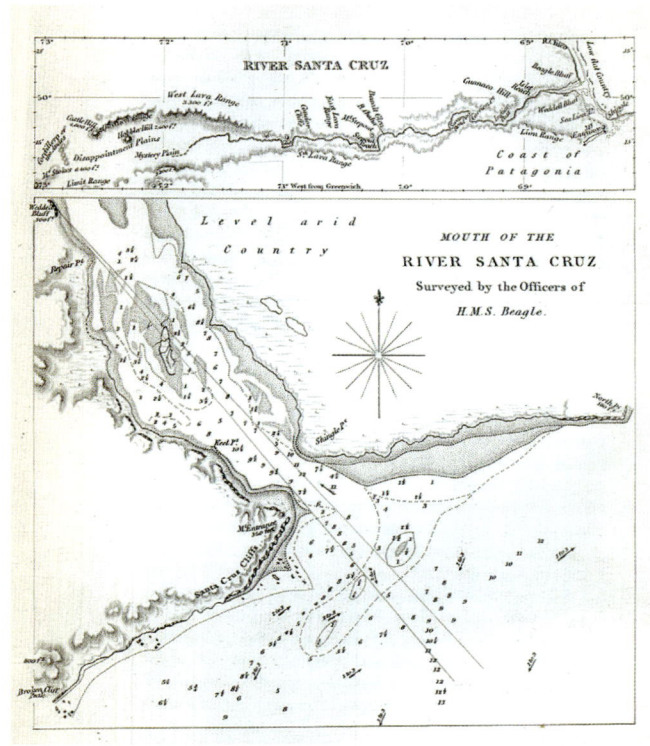

April 22nd

"The country remained the same, and was extremely uninteresting. The complete similarity of the productions throughout Patagonia is one of its most striking characters. The level plains of arid shingle support the same stunted and dwarf plants; and in the valleys the same thorn-bearing bushes grow. Everywhere we see the same birds and insects.

Even the very banks of the river and of the clear streamlets which entered it, were scarcely enlivened by a brighter tint of green. The curse of sterility is on the land, and the water flowing over a bed of pebbles partakes of the same curse. Hence the number of waterfowl is very scanty; for there is nothing to support life in the stream of this barren river.

(...) The guanaco is also in his proper district; herds of fifty or a hundred were common; and, as I have stated, we saw one which must have contained at least five hundred."

April 27th

"(...) This day I shot a condor. It measured from tip to tip of the wings, eight and a half feet, and from beak to tail, four feet. This bird is known to have a wide geographical range. (...)

When the condors are wheeling in a flock round and round any spot, their flight is beautiful. Except when rising from the ground, I do not recollect ever having seen one of these birds flap its wings."

May 4th

"Captain FitzRoy determined to take the boats no higher. The river had a winding course, and was very rapid; and the appearance of the country offered no temptation to proceed any further. Everywhere we met with the same productions, and the same dreary landscape. We were now one hundred and forty miles distant from the Atlantic, and about sixty from the nearest arm of the Pacific. The valley in this upper part expanded into a wide basin, bounded on the north and south by the basaltic platforms, and fronted by the long range of the snow-clad Cordillera. But we viewed these grand mountains with regret, for we were obliged to imagine their nature. (...) Besides the useless loss of time which an attempt to ascend the river any higher would have cost us, we had already been for some days on half allowance of bread."

This is as far as Darwin and FitzRoy sailed on the Santa Cruz River. The plaque left by Gerardo Bartolomé and other expeditionary members in December 2003 represented a small treasure hunt for me and the F 800 GS.
If the Beagle crew members had walked two more hours, the Argentino Lake could probably be called FitzRoy Lake today.

Good Success Bay in Tierra del Fuego *

54° 48' 02" S
65° 14' 00" W

December 17th, 1832

"Having now finished with Patagonia and the Falkland Islands, I will describe our first arrival in Tierra del Fuego. A little after noon we doubled Cape San Diego, and entered the famous strait of Le Maire. We kept close to the Fuegian shore, but the outline of the rugged, inhospitable Staten-land was visible amidst the clouds. In the afternoon we anchored in the Bay of Good Success. While entering we were saluted in a manner becoming the inhabitants of this savage land. A group of Fuegians partly concealed by the entangled forest, were perched on a wild point overhanging the sea; and as we passed by, they sprang up and waving their tattered cloaks sent forth a loud and sonorous shout. The savages followed the ship, and just before dark we saw their fire, and again heard their wild cry. The harbour consists of a fine piece of water half surrounded by low rounded mountains of clay-slate, which are covered to the water's edge by one dense gloomy forest. A single glance at the landscape was sufficient to show me how widely different it was from any thing I had ever beheld. At night it blew a gale of wind, and heavy squalls from the mountains swept past us. It would have been a bad time out at sea, and we, as well as others, may call this Good Success Bay."

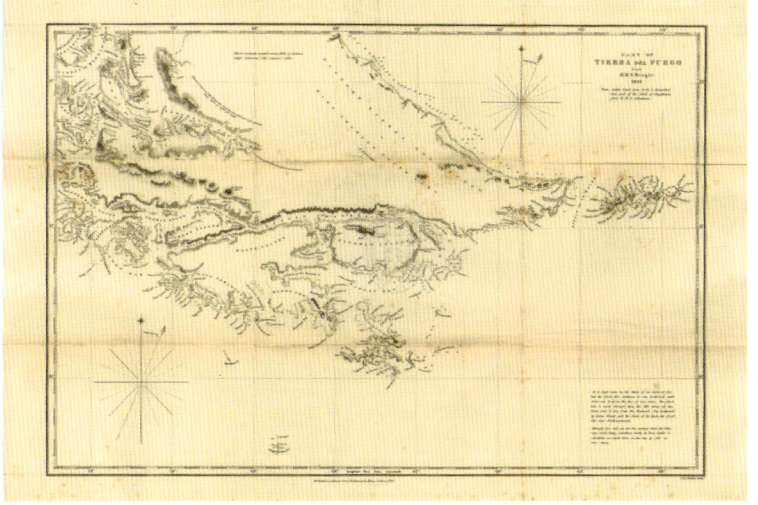

* Editor's note: following the order and
chronology in Darwin's original Journal,
this chapter leads us back to the year 1832.

1832-2010

Today, Good Success Bay is a small permanent post from the Argentine Armada, with five marines with different specialties. One of their main duties is to control the crossing of ships through the Le Maire Strait towards Ushuaia. There is no access by land, save for some isolated successful expedition, therefore the only possible access is by sea. In the event of a storm, it still stands as an important shelter for all sorts of vessels. Regarding the history this book traces, Good Success is an essential place and represents in a faithful way an event that will repeat itself on the pages that illustrate Navarino and other places in Tierra del Fuego which is the presence of Fueguinos (natives). For this and other reasons, setting foot on its coast fills us with emotion and pride.

Cape Horn

December 21st

"(...) Favoured to an uncommon degree by a fine easterly breeze, we closed in with the Barnevelts, and running past Cape Deceit with its stony peaks, about three o'clock doubled the weather-beaten Cape Horn. The evening was calm and bright, and we enjoyed a fine view of the surrounding isles. Cape Horn, however, demanded his tribute, and before night sent us a gale of wind directly in our teeth."

C.D.

One of the famous stops on board the Via Australis Cruise between Punta Arenas and Ushuaia is Cape Horn. Disembarking (the actual possibility or not) depends on the weather. Darwin had no luck; we did.

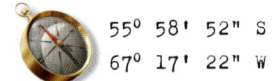
55° 58' 52" S
67° 17' 22" W

The southernmost part of Hornos Island. This cape was considered, for centuries, the end of the world; and it possibly still is. The same rocks that have seen many dreams go under, offer us an incredible and unique view.

a BMW F 800 GS
at the end of the world

Caleta Eugenia, Seno Goeree   54° 55' 51.5" S
67° 17' 03.3" W

Isla Navarino. The last chance I have to ride my motorbike in the southern south. The road finishes at the gates of Estancia Eugenia, but the person in charge allows me to cross the land up to the cove's extreme, and in this way arrive at the southernmost part a rider has ever reached. Only a BMW made it so far.

Woollya Bay. This part of the island was home to Jemmy Button's tribe. This is where Captain FitzRoy disembarked three "Fueguinos" who travelled on board the Beagle, together with Reverend Matthews. The mission failed. Jemmy's own relatives stole from him all the belongings he had brought from England. York and Fuegía ran away and the ashamed Reverend decided to settle in New Zealand and start all over, far away from these wild lands.

Woollya
Two centuries later, a new disembarkation

There are no "Fueguinos" left in Woollya. It is possible, however, to relive the past thanks to the Australis and its Mare, Via and Stella Cruises. On the way to Cape Horn, the historical bay on the island of Navarino is one of the most exciting points of attraction during the journey.

January 1833

"Jemmy was now in a district well known to him, and guided the boats to a quiet pretty cove named Woollya (...) The cove was bordered by some acres of good sloping land, not covered (as elsewhere) either by peat or by forest-trees. Although it was not the place where Fuegía Basket and York Minster lived, they all decided to stay there, including Matthews, the missionary. Five days were spent in building for them three large wigwams, in landing their goods, in digging two gardens, and sowing seeds."

C.D.

The only construction on this part of the island is a museum, where the Atlantis Cruises keep Woollya's history alive. Captain FitzRoy has his own monolith and a pod of dolphins watching over it.

Navarino Island today

Following Darwin to the summit of Tarn Mount
1834-2010

"When the Beagle was here in the month of February, I started one morning at four o'clock to ascend Mount Tarn, which is 2600 feet high, and is the most elevated point in this immediate district. We went in a boat to the foot of the mountain (but unluckily not to the best part), and then began our ascent. The forest commences at the line of high-water mark, and during the first two hours I gave over all hopes of reaching the summit. (…)

In the deep ravines, the death-like scene of desolation exceeded all description."

C.D.

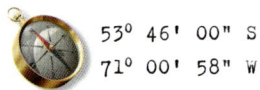

53° 46' 00" S
71° 00' 58" W

We at last found ourselves among the stunted trees, and then soon reached the bare ridge, which conducted us to the summit. Here was a view characteristic of Tierra del Fuego; irregular chains of hills, mottled with patches of snow, deep yellowish-green valleys, and arms of the sea intersecting the land in many directions."

Strait of Magellan

June 1st

"We anchored in the fine bay of Port Famine. It was now the beginning of winter, and I never saw a more cheerless prospect; the dusky woods, piebald with snow, could be only seen indistinctly through a drizzling hazy atmosphere. We were, however, lucky in getting two fine days."

Port Famine (Puerto del Hambre) has slightly changed since the H.M.S. Beagle visit. The principal bay is a small fishing port. The neighbouring bay silently watches over memorial plaques to this unlucky town founded by Sarmiento de Gamboa in 1584. Thanks to the visit of the Spanish Frigate, Elcano, the monument was restored by the Armada of Chile.

When the H.M.S. Beagle arrived on these coasts, it anchored in a bay not far from the Spanish settlement in Port Famine. In this bay, there is a compulsory stop for any traveler keen on the story here narrated: the tomb of the first H.M.S. Beagle's captain Pringle Stokes. Overwhelmed by the pressures of time and deadlines, and aware of the probability of having to spend another winter sailing the Magellan Strait and other channels, he shot himself in 1828. He was replaced by lieutenant Robert FitzRoy. Stokes' dramatic decision unchained one of the most important events of the Century. Who would have thought that years later Captain FitzRoy would have the same ending?
When the Beagle visited Port Famine, it anchored in this same bay.

San Isidro's Lighthouse

 53° 47' 5.95" S
70° 58' 29.76" W

Cape San Isidro and Cape Froward (a few kilometers from there) are the southernmost points in the American Continent. Charles Darwin walked these coasts and from a bay next to the lighthouse, climbed the Tarn Mount.

The San Isidro Lodge can be found in this same bay. It is the place to stop if one wants to trace back FitzRoy and Darwin's stops in this area, since it is located near Tarn Mount. The woods and the coast look exactly the same way they did back in 1834. The view of the strait from the lodge is unique and gives the sensation of being at the end of the world.

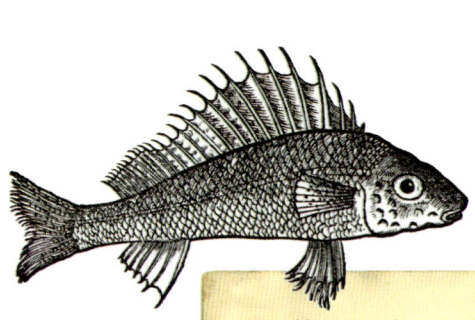

On its way through the Magellan Strait, the Mexican Frigate Cuauhtémoc (three times the size of the H.M.S. Beagle) tricked me into believing, at times, that Captain FitzRoy and Charles Darwin had come back.

"It is a curious fact to notice the multiplication —extraordinary fast— of the horse in South America. These animals were debarked in Buenos Aires in 1537 for the first time, and as the colony has been abandoned for some time, the horse turned wild. In 1580, only 43 years after, you can see them in the Magellan Strait!".

C.D.

Sandy Point

One of the most important events after the Beagle's visit to Magellan Strait in 1834 was the founding of the Chilean city of Sandy Point (Punta Arenas). Captain FitzRoy and other English knew this place as Sandy Point. This is where its name derived from some years later, when Governor José Santos Mardones decided to move the population from Bulnes Fortress to this location. The new town was born on December 18th, 1848.

The city turned into the center of trade in Patagonia, centralizing stock breeding, mining and sea transport. José Nogueira and his wife, Sara Braun, José Menéndez and his daughter Josefina Menéndez Behety (married to Sara's brother, Mauricio) left, each at their time, an indelible legacy in this city.

The Fuegian Channels

We live in a fascinating era! On board
the Via Australis the inanimate works of
nature do not seem as scary as Charles
Darwin describes them.

June 8th

"We weighed anchor early in the morning and left Port Famine. Captain Fitz Roy determined to leave the Strait of Magellan by the Magdalen Channel, which had not long been discovered. Our course lay due south, down that gloomy passage which I have before alluded to, as appearing to lead to another and worse world. The wind was fair, but the atmosphere was very thick; so that we missed much curious scenery. The dark ragged clouds were rapidly driven over the mountains, from their summits nearly down to their bases. The glimpses which we caught through the dusky mass, were highly interesting; jagged points, cones of snow, blue glaciers, strong outlines, marked on a lurid sky, were seen at different distances and heights. (...)

The inanimate works of nature –rock, ice, snow, wind, and water– all warring with each other, yet combined against man, here reigned in absolute sovereignty."

C.D.

Darwin told us before that "the inanimate works of nature all warring with each other, yet combined against man —here reigned in absolute sovereignty". Today, almost 200 years later, we would call this "collateral damage", and no doubt the great victims of this fight were the "Fueguinos", who were completely wiped out. The coming of the "civilized" man to these lands had a lot to do with it. To Darwin's list (rock, ice, snow, wind, water) colonizers could also be added. Eugenio Calderón (picture) is the son of Cristina, the last pure Yagana left on the planet. He is 81 years old and lives in Williams Port. I took this portrait in the same Magdalena Channel where Charles predicted the uneven result between these tremendous forces.

The "Bahía Azul" ferry, from Austral Broom, is an essential link between Punta Arenas and Navarino Island. Its route covers the same channels the H.M.S. Beagle sailed two centuries ago.

"Several glaciers descended in a winding course from the upper great expanse of snow to the sea-coast: they may be likened to great frozen Niagaras; and perhaps these cataracts of blue ice are full as beautiful as the moving ones of water"

C.D.

Central Chile

July 23rd

"The Beagle anchored late at night in the bay of Valparaíso, the chief seaport of Chile. When morning came, everything appeared delightful. After Tierra del Fuego, the climate felt quite delicious –the atmosphere so dry, and the heavens so clear and blue with the sun shining brightly, that all nature seemed sparkling with life. The view from the anchorage is very pretty. The town is built at the very foot of a range of hills, about 1.600 feet high, and rather steep. From its position, it consists of one long, straggling street, which runs parallel to the beach, and wherever a ravine comes down, the houses are piled up on each side of it.

(…) I had the good fortune to find living here Mister Richard Corfield, an old schoolfellow and friend, to whose hospitality and kindness I was greatly indebted, in having afforded me a most pleasant residence during the Beagle's stay in Chile."

Valparaíso is one of the most beautiful cities in Chile. Its architecture spreads amongst bays and hills, and every corner resembles a painting.

"I did not cease from wonder at finding each succeeding day as fine as the foregoing. What a difference does climate make in the enjoyment of life!

C.D.

August 1834, Valparaiso.

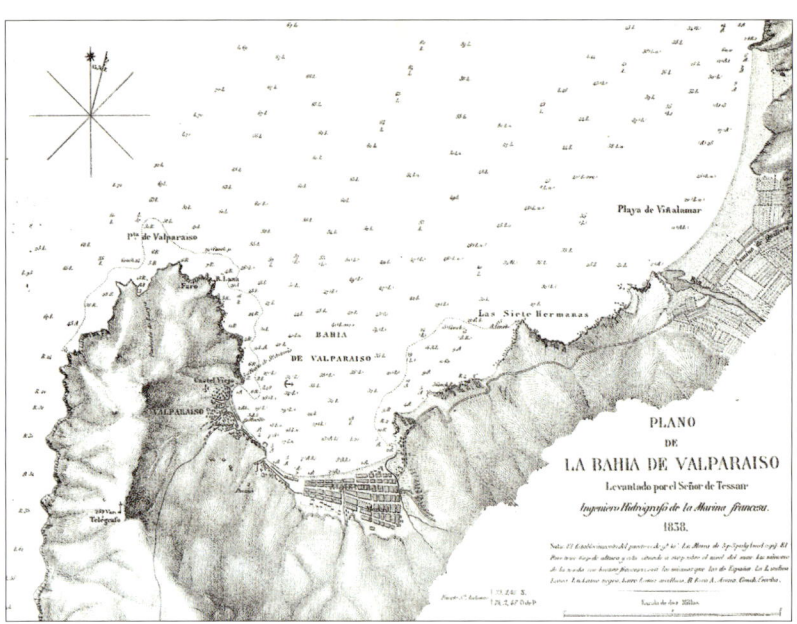

As from 1536, with the coming of the Spanish Diego de Almagro, Valparaíso hosted visitors of all sorts: from the not very romantic pirates who were very interested in gold from Perú, to adventurers like Darwin who found the city fascinating. This last sensation hasn't changed at all.

Valparaiso Surroundings

August 1834 - Quillota Valley

"I set out on a riding excursion, for the purpose of geologising the basal parts of the Andes, which alone at this time of the year are not shut up by the winter snow. Our first day's ride was northward along the sea-coast. After dark we reached the Hacienda of Quintero, the estate which formerly belonged to Lord Cochrane. (…)"

"The valley of Quillota is very broad and quite flat, and is thus easily irrigated in all parts. The little square gardens are crowded with orange and olive trees, and every sort of vegetable. On each side huge bare mountains rise, and this from the contrast renders the patchwork valley the more pleasing. Whoever called 'Valparaíso, the valley of Paradise', must have been thinking of Quillota."

C.D.

Ascent to La Campana Mount

"The mayor-domo of the Hacienda was good enough to give me a guide and fresh horses; and in the morning we set out to ascend the Campana, or Bell Mountain, which is 6.400 feet high. The paths were very bad, but both the geology and scenery amply repaid the trouble."

The sign to honour the century of Darwin's ascent to La Campana Mount. It was donated by the Scientific Society of Valparaíso and the British Community.

We spent the day on the summit, and I never enjoyed one more thoroughly. Chile, bounded by the Andes and the Pacific, was seen as in a map. The pleasure from the scenery, in itself beautiful, was heightened by the many reflections which arose from the mere view of the Campana range (…)

Who can avoid wondering at the force which has upheaved these mountains, and even more so at the countless ages which it must have required, to have broken through, removed, and levelled whole masses of them?

We must not now reverse the wonder, and doubt whether all-powerful time can grind down mountains –even the gigantic Cordillera– into gravel and mud."

Cauquenes Hotbaths

September 6th

"We proceeded due south, and slept at Rancagua. The road passed over the level but narrow plain, bounded on one side by lofty hills, and on the other by the Cordillera. The next day we turned up the valley of the Río Cachapual, in which the hotbaths of Cauquenes, long celebrated for their medicinal properties, are situated. (Editor's note: General San Martín enjoyed its benefits twice while he was fighting for independence, first in 1820 and then in 1822).

The mineral springs of Cauquenes burst forth on a line of dislocation, crossing a mass of stratified rock, the whole of which betrays the action of heat. A considerable quantity of gas is continually escaping from the same orifices with the water. Though the springs are only a few yards apart, they have very different temperatures; and this appears to be the result of an unequal mixture of cold water: for those with the lowest temperature have scarcely any mineral taste. After the great earthquake of 1822 the springs ceased, and the water did not return for nearly a year."

Two weeks before visiting these thermal springs, a big earthquake hard-hit the center of Chile. The moment I took these pictures, water had stopped to flow as a consequence of the tremor.

One day I rode up the valley to the farthest inhabited spot. Shortly above that point, the Cachapual divides into two deep tremendous ravines, which penetrate directly into the great range. I scrambled up a peaked mountain, probably more than six thousand feet high. Here, as indeed everywhere else, scenes of the highest interest presented themselves. It was by one of these ravines, that Pincheira entered Chile and ravaged the neighbouring country. This is the same man whose attack on an estancia at the Rio Negro I have described. He was a renegade half-cast Spaniard, who collected a great body of Indians together and established himself by a stream in the Pampas, which place none of the forces sent after him could ever discover. From this point he used to sally forth, and crossing the Cordillera by passes hitherto unattempted, he ravaged the farm-houses and drove the cattle to his secret rendezvous. Pincheira was a capital horseman, and he made all around him equally good, for he invariably shot any one who hesitated to follow him. It was against this man, and other wandering Indian tribes, that Rosas waged the war of extermination."

C.D.

Yaquil Mines

September 13th

"We left the baths of Cauquenes, and rejoining the main road slept at the Rio Claro. From this place we rode to the town of San Fernando. Before arriving there, the last land-locked basin had expanded into a great plain, which extended so far to the south, that the snowy summits of the more distant Andes were seen as if above the horizon of the sea. San Fernando is forty leagues from Santiago; and it was my farthest point southward; for we here turned at right angles towards the coast. We slept at the gold-mines of Yaquil, which are worked by Mr. Nixon, an American gentleman, to whose kindness I was much indebted during the four days I stayed at his house. The next morning we rode to the mines, which are situated at the distance of some leagues, near the summit of a lofty hill."

Yaquil Mines were hard to
find, since I couldn't find
a single native person who
had heard about them.

The only golden thing I found was the grace of its inhabitants, who in spite of the consequences suffered from the earthquake that destroyed everything weeks before, hadn't lost their hopes and morale.

Chiloé and Chonos Islands

November 10th

"The Beagle sailed from Valparaíso to the south, for the purpose of surveying the southern part of Chile, the island of Chiloé, and the broken land called the Chonos Archipelago, as far south as the Península of Tres Montes. On the 21st we anchored in the bay of San Carlos, the capital of Chiloé." (Editor's Note: today Ancud)

"This island is about ninety miles long, with a breadth of rather less than thirty. The land is hilly, but not mountainous, and is covered by one great forest, except where a few green patches have been cleared round the thatched cottages. From a distance the view somewhat resembles that of Tierra del Fuego; but the woods, when seen nearer, are incomparably more beautiful. Many kinds of fine evergreen trees, and plants with a tropical character, here take the place of the gloomy beech of the southern shores. In winter the climate is detestable, and in summer it is only a little better. I should think there are few parts of the world, within the temperate regions, where so much rain falls. The winds are very boisterous, and the sky almost always clouded: to have a week of fine weather is something wonderful." (...)

"The inhabitants, from their complexion and low stature, appear to have three-fourths of Indian blood in their veins. They are an humble, quiet, industrious set of men"

C.D.

There is very little pasture for the larger quadrupeds; and in consequence, the staple articles of food are pigs, potatoes, and fish. (…)
The forests are so impenetrable, that the land is nowhere cultivated except near the coast and on the adjoining islets."

November 24th

"The yawl and whale-boat were sent under the command of Mr. (now Captain) Sulivan, to survey the eastern or inland coast of Chiloe; and with orders to meet the Beagle at the southern extremity of the island; to which point she would proceed by the outside, so as thus to circumnavigate the whole. I accompanied this expedition, but instead of going in the boats the first day, I hired horses to take me to Chacao, at the northern extremity of the island. The road followed the coast; every now and then crossing promontories covered by fine forests. In these shaded paths it is absolutely necessary that the whole road should be made of logs of wood, which are squared and placed by the side of each other."

Between the city of Ancud (formerly San Carlos) and Chacao there is a biological station called Senda Darwin (Darwin's Path). It preserves the same original road the English scientist took, and teaches its meaning.

The land in this neighbourhood has been extensively cleared, and there were many quiet and most picturesque nooks in the forest. Chacao was formerly the principal port in the island; but many vessels having been lost, owing to the dangerous currents and rocks in the straits, the Spanish government burnt the church, and thus arbitrarily compelled the greater number of inhabitants to migrate to San Carlos. We had not long bivouacked, before the barefooted son of the governor came down to reconnoitre us."

November 30th

"Early on Sunday morning we reached Castro, the ancient capital of Chiloé, but now a most forlorn and deserted place. The usual quadrangular arrangement of Spanish towns could be traced, but the streets and plaza were coated with fine green turf, on which sheep were browsing. The church, which stands in the middle, is entirely built of plank, and has a picturesque and venerable appearance. The poverty of the place may be conceived from the fact, that although containing some hundreds of inhabitants, one of our party was unable anywhere to purchase either a pound of sugar or an ordinary knife. No individual possessed either a watch or a clock; and an old man, who was supposed to have a good idea of time, was employed to strike the church bell by guess."

December 1st

"We steered for the island of Lemuy. I was anxious to examine a reported coal-mine, which turned out to be lignite of little value (…) The people here live chiefly on shell-fish and potatoes. At certain seasons they catch also, in "corrales," or hedges under water, many fish which are left on the mud-banks as the tide falls. They occasionally possess fowls, sheep, goats, pigs, horses, and cattle; the order in which they are here mentioned, expressing their respective numbers."

C.D.

Valdivia & Niebla Fort

February, 1835

"We steered northward along shore, but owing to thick weather did not reach Valdivia till the night of the 8th. The next morning the boat proceeded to the town, which is distant about ten miles. We followed the course of the river, occasionally passing a few hovels, and patches of ground cleared out of the otherwise unbroken forest (…)

The town is so completely buried in a wood of apple-trees that the streets are merely paths in an orchard."

A few days afterwards I crossed the bay with a party of officers, and landed near the fort called Niebla. The buildings were in a most ruinous state, and the gun-carriages quite rotten. Mr. Wickham remarked to the commanding officer, that with one discharge they would certainly all fall to pieces. The poor man, trying to put a good face upon it, gravely replied, "No, I am sure, sir, they would stand two!" The Spaniards must have intended to have made this place impregnable. There is now lying in the middle of the courtyard a little mountain of mortar, which rivals in hardness the rock on which it is placed. It was brought from Chile, and cost 7.000 dollars. The revolution having broken out, prevented its being applied to any purpose, and now it remains a monument of the fallen greatness of Spain."

Earthquake in Valdivia, Concepción & Talcahuano

February 20th, 1835

"This day has been memorable in the annals of Valdivia, for the most severe earthquake experienced by the oldest inhabitant. I happened to be on shore, and was lying down in the wood to rest myself. It came on suddenly, and lasted two minutes, but the time appeared much longer. (…)

A bad earthquake at once destroys our oldest associations: the earth, the very emblem of solidity, has moved beneath our feet like a thin crust over a fluid;—one second of time has created in the mind a strange idea of insecurity, which hours of reflection would not have produced. In the forest, as a breeze moved the trees, I felt only the earth tremble, but saw no other effect. Captain FitzRoy and some officers were at the town during the shock, and there the scene was more striking."

March 5th

"I landed at Talcahuano, and afterwards rode to Concepción. Both towns presented the most awful yet interesting spectacle I ever beheld. To a person who had formerly known them, it possibly might have been still more impressive; for the ruins were so mingled together."

It is generally thought that this has been the worst earthquake ever recorded in Chile; but as the very severe ones occur only after long intervals, this cannot easily be known; nor indeed would a much worse shock have made any great difference, for the ruin was now complete. Innumerable small tremblings followed the great earthquake, and within the first twelve days no less than three hundred were counted."

"In Talcahuano, shortly after the shock, a great wave was seen from the distance of three or four miles, approaching in the middle of the bay with a smooth outline. (…) A schooner was left in the midst of the ruins, 200 yards from the beach. In one part of the bay, a ship was pitched high and dry on shore, was carried off, again driven on shore, and again carried off."

"It is a bitter and humiliating thing to see works, which have cost man so much time and labour, overthrown in one minute; yet compassion for the inhabitants was almost instantly banished, by the surprise in seeing a state of things produced in a moment of time, which one was accustomed to attribute to a succession of ages."

C.D.

Crossing the Cordillera: going through El Portillo and returning by Uspallata

"On the 11th we anchored at Valparaíso, and two days afterwards I set out to cross the Cordillera. I proceeded to Santiago, where Mr. Caldcleugh most kindly assisted me in every possible way in making the little preparations which were necessary. In this part of Chile there are two passes across the Andes to Mendoza: the one most commonly used—namely, that of Aconcagua or Uspallata—is situated some way to the north; the other, called the Portillo, is to the south, and nearer, but more lofty and dangerous."

(Editor's note: The Portillo Pass that Darwin refers to is an old trail for mules, that begins near Tupungato City in Mendoza).

March 18th

"We set out for the Portillo pass. Leaving Santiago we crossed the wide burnt-up plain on which that city stands, and in the afternoon arrived at the Maypu, one of the principal rivers in Chile (…)

In the evening we passed the custom-house, where our luggage was examined. The custom-house officers were very civil, which was perhaps partly owing to the passport which the President of the Republic had given me; but I must express my admiration at the natural politeness of almost every Chileno. I may mention an anecdote with which I was at the time much pleased: we met near Mendoza a little and very fat negress, riding astride on a mule. She had a goître so enormous that it was scarcely possible to avoid gazing at her for a moment; but my two companions almost instantly, by way of apology, made the common salute of the country by taking off their hats."

March 19th

"We rode during this day to the last, and therefore most elevated house in the valley. The number of inhabitants became scanty; but wherever water could be brought on the land, it was very fertile."

Darwin in Mendoza: Portillo Pass (4.300 meters)

March 1835 – Cordillera de los Andes

"Our manner of travelling was delightfully independent. In the inhabited parts we bought a little firewood, hired pasture for the animals, and bivouacked in the corner of the same field with them. Carrying an iron pot, we cooked and ate our supper under a cloudless sky, and knew no trouble. My companions were Mariano Gonzales, who had formerly accompanied me in Chile, and an "arriero," with his ten mules and a "madrina." The madrina (or godmother) is a most important personage: she is an old steady mare, with a little bell round her neck; and wherever she goes, the mules, like good children, follow her. The affection of these animals for their madrinas saves infinite trouble. If several large troops are turned into one field to graze, in the morning the muleteers have only to lead the madrinas a little apart, and tinkle their bells; and although there may be two or three hundred together, each mule immediately knows the bell of its own madrina, and comes to her.

(…) Yet with what delicate slim limbs, without any proportional bulk of muscle, these animals support so great a burden! That a hybrid should possess more reason, memory, obstinacy, social affection, powers of muscular endurance, and length of life, than either of its parents, seems to indicate that art has here outdone nature."

March 21st

"Having crossed the Peuquenes, we descended into a mountainous country, intermediate between the two main ranges, and then took up our quarters for the night. We were now in the republic of Mendoza. The elevation was probably not under 11.000 feet, and the vegetation in consequence exceedingly scanty. (...)

At the place where we slept water necessarily boiled, from the diminished pressure of the atmosphere, at a lower temperature than it does in a less lofty country; the case being the converse of that of a Papin's digester. Hence the potatoes, after remaining for some hours in the boiling water, were nearly as hard as ever. The pot was left on the fire all night, and next morning it was boiled again, but yet the potatoes were not cooked. I found out this, by overhearing my two companions discussing the cause; they had come to the simple conclusion, 'that the cursed pot (which was a new one) did not choose to boil potatoes'."

March 22nd

"After eating our potato-less breakfast, we travelled across the intermediate tract to the foot of the Portillo range. In the middle of summer cattle are brought up here to graze; but they had now all been removed.
We had a fine view of a mass of mountains called Tupungato, the whole clothed with unbroken snow."

"When nearly on the crest of the Portillo, we were enveloped in a falling cloud of minute frozen spicula. This was very unfortunate, as it continued the whole day, and quite intercepted our view. The pass takes its name of Portillo, from a narrow cleft or doorway on the highest ridge, through which the road passes."

C.D.

Marcelo Caetano has been leading horseback rides for many years. He guides groups across the Andes. The habit of offering something to the mountain is still carried out.

On trip to Luján de Cuyo

March 25th

"The road proceeded for some distance due east across a low swamp; then meeting the dry plain, it turned to the north towards Mendoza.

Our first day's journey was called fourteen leagues to Estacado, and the second seventeen to Luxan, near Mendoza. The whole distance is over a level desert plain, with not more than two or three houses.

There is very little water in this "traversia," and in our second day's journey we found only one little pool. Little water flows from the mountains, and it soon becomes absorbed by the dry and porous soil."

Much has changed in this part of Luján since Charles Darwin came here 175 ago. Finca La Anita is a clear evidence of agricultural evolution derived from the handling of watering channels and irrigation ditches during the last hundred years.

We crossed the Luxan (Editor's note: today called Mendoza), which is a river of considerable size, though its course towards the sea-coast is very imperfectly known: it is even doubtful whether, in passing over the plains, it is not evaporated and lost. We slept in the village of Luxan, which is a small place surrounded by gardens.
At night I experienced an attack (for it deserves no less a name) of the Benchuca, a species of Reduvius, the great black bug of the Pampas."

March 27th

"We rode on to Mendoza. The country was beautifully cultivated, and resembled Chile. This neighbourhood is celebrated for its fruit; and certainly nothing could appear more flourishing than the vineyards and the orchards of figs, peaches, and olives. We bought water-melons nearly twice as large as a man's head, most deliciously cool and well-flavoured."

C.D.

Charles Darwin in Villa Vicencio, Mendoza

March 29th - Uspallata hill (sierra)

"We set out on our return to Chile, by the Uspallata pass situated north of Mendoza. We had to cross a long and most sterile traversia of fifteen leagues. The soil in parts was absolutely bare, in others covered by numberless dwarf cacti, armed with formidable spines, and called by the inhabitants "little lions." (…)

Before sunset we entered one of the wide valleys, or rather bays, which open on the plain: this soon narrowed into a ravine, where a little higher up the house of Villa Vicencio is situated. As we had ridden all day without a drop of water, both our mules and selves were very thirsty, and we looked out anxiously for the stream which flows down this valley. It was curious to observe how gradually the water made its appearance: on the plain the course was quite dry; by degrees it became a little damper; then puddles of water appeared; these soon became connected; and at Villa Vicencio there was a nice little rivulet."

The virtues of Villavicencio Springs have been acknowledged for several centuries. It is a spring of healing waters, a place for travelers to rest, and thermal baths.
Today, its water travels through kilometers of stainless steel pipes to be bottled in a model plant outside the National Park.

Paramillos Petrified Woods

March 30th

"The solitary hovel which bears the imposing name of Villa Vicencio, has been mentioned by every traveller who has crossed the Andes. I stayed here and at some neighbouring mines during the two succeeding days. (…)The Uspallata range has nearly the same geographical position with respect to the Cordillera, which the gigantic Portillo line has, but it is of a totally different origin: it consists of various kinds of submarine lava, alternating with volcanic sandstones and other remarkable sedimentary deposits; the whole having a very close resemblance to some of the tertiary beds on the shores of the Pacific. From this resemblance I expected to find silicified wood, which is generally characteristic of those formations. I was gratified in a very extraordinary manner. In the central part of the range, at an elevation of about seven thousand feet, I observed on a bare slope some snow-white projecting columns. These were petrified trees (...)

The volcanic sandstone in which the trees were embedded, and from the lower part of which they must have sprung, had accumulated in successive thin layers around their trunks; and the stone yet retained the impression of the bark. It required little geological practice to interpret the marvellous story which this scene at once unfolded; though I confess I was at first so much astonished, that I could scarcely believe the plainest evidence. I saw the spot where a cluster of fine trees once waved their branches on the shores of the Atlantic, when that ocean (now driven back 700 miles) came to the foot of the Andes."

C.D.

The BMW key points at a petrified branch from faraway times. These stone "Araucarias" are disseminated all over the area but are not easily distinguishable, since many of the trunks were taken from this place and only the impressions on the rocks remain. This huge discovery gave Darwin a clear vision of the origin of the Andes.

Las Vacas River

April 2nd, 1835 – On the way to Chile

(...) "We reached the Río de las Vacas, which is considered the worst stream in the Cordillera to cross. As all these rivers have a rapid and short course, and are formed by the melting of the snow, the hour of the day makes a considerable difference in their volume. In the evening the stream is muddy and full, but about daybreak it becomes clearer and much less impetuous. This we found to be the case with the Río de las Vacas, and in the morning we crossed it with little difficulty."

This picture was taken on March 9th, 2010 at 7:50 AM, and I suppose it looks exactly the same way Charles saw it when he came here at this same time of the year. The big difference lies on the two bridges (the old and the new) at the background over Route 7.

"The scenery thus far was very uninteresting, compared with that of the Portillo pass. Little can be seen beyond the bare walls of the one grand, flat-bottomed valley, which the road follows up to the highest crest. The valley and the huge rocky mountains are extremely barren: during the two previous nights the poor mules had absolutely nothing to eat, for excepting a few low resinous bushes, scarcely a plant can be seen. In the course of this day we crossed some of the worst passes in the Cordillera, but their danger has been much exaggerated. I was told that if I attempted to pass on foot, my head would turn giddy."

C.D.

Incas Bridge

April 4th

"From the Río de las Vacas to the Puente del Incas, half a day's journey. As there was pasture for the mules, and geology for me, we bivouacked here for the night. When one hears of a natural Bridge, one pictures to oneself some deep and narrow ravine, across which a bold mass of rock has fallen; or a great arch hollowed out like the vault of a cavern. Instead of this, the Incas Bridge consists of a crust of stratified shingle, cemented together by the deposits of the neighbouring hot springs.

It appears, as if the stream had scooped out a channel on one side, leaving an overhanging ledge, which was met by earth and stones falling down from the opposite cliff. Certainly an oblique junction, as would happen in such a case, was very distinct on one side. The Bridge of the Incas is by no means worthy of the great monarchs whose name it bears."

C.D.

Valley of the Aconcagua

April 5th

"We had a long day's ride across the central ridge, from the Incas Bridge to the Ojos del Agua, which are situated near the lowest casucha on the Chilian side. (…) The scenery was grand: to the westward there was a fine chaos of mountains, divided by profound ravines. The sky was cloudless, excepting a few round little masses of vapour, that floated over the highest pinnacles."

Many times in his journals Darwin makes reference to the giant of America but under the name of Aconcagua Volcano. I took this picture of the Horcones Valley in previous journeys, but it was the triggering inspiration for this adventure, and this is why it deserves a place in this book.

Leaving the Cordillera behind: heading for Santiago

April 8th

"We left the valley of the Aconcagua, by which we had descended, and reached in the evening a cottage near the Villa de Santa Rosa. The fertility of the plain was delightful: the autumn being advanced, the leaves of many of the fruit-trees were falling; and of the labourers,—some were busy in drying figs and peaches on the roofs of their cottages, while others were gathering the grapes from the vineyards. It was a pretty scene; but I missed that pensive stillness which makes the autumn in England indeed the evening of the year. On the 10th we reached Santiago, where I received a very kind and hospitable reception from Mr. Caldcleugh. My excursion only cost me twenty-four days, and never did I more deeply enjoy an equal space of time."

C.D.

Returning to England
Copiapó, Lima, Galápagos

After crossing the Andes, Charles Darwin returned to Valparaíso.

On April 27th, 1835 –with FitzRoy's approval– he prepared a new journey northwards. The plan was to cover 700 kilometers by land up to Copiapó and there he would go on board the Beagle again.

In order to make this trip he hired new guides, bought four horses and two mules (for which he paid 25 pounds) and with his habitual independence he set off. He visited Quillota, Conchalí, Los Hornos and Coquimbo. There he coincided with the Beagle, on its voyage through the Pacific, and together with FitzRoy they ate at the house of an Englishman called Mr. Edwards. He then followed towards Huasco and finally arrived in Copiapó. Both times he covered the Andes with excellent results for his investigations on the formation of these mountains. Some days before boarding the ship, he sold all six animals for 23 pounds and recovered his investment.

For a period of two months (he boarded the H.M.S. Beagle on July, 5th), Darwin visited copper and silver mines, Indian ruins, removed stones, found fossils and filled his brown leathered journals with hundreds of notes like this:

"I have got convincing proofs that this part of the South American continent has raised about 400 to 500 feet near the coast and even 1.000 to 1.300 feet, in some parts, from the time the existing shells lived. Towards the mountain, the elevation has probably been bigger. Just like the peculiar aridity of the weather is a clear consequence of the height in the Andes, there is the certainty that before these elevations existed, the weather was more humid."

From Copiapó, together with Captain FitzRoy, they sailed towards Iquique and then to Del Callao Port, in Lima, Peru. They stayed there for fifty days, but due to problems known to the public, it was very little what they covered. His descriptions on this stage had to do with the weather, the people and some markets they visited.

On September, 7th the return to England would begin, sailing through Polynesia and New Zealand. They had to cross the Pacific stopping at Galápagos Islands; possibly, the most famous stops of all, but not part of our journey…

Copiapó and other places Darwin visited in the
North of Chile have been the setting to the famous
Dakar race, that has taken place for the last three
years in Argentina and Chile. Maybe without knowing
it, millions of TV viewers watched directly the
same landscapes Charles toured two centuries ago.

Back home

Darwin returned to England on board the H.M.S. Beagle after 1.740 days of voyage. Our journey was more modest and only lasted 64 days.

However, some numbers given by the F 800 GS speak about the small adventure implied in the making of this book across three countries.

14.663 kilometers on motorcycle
and **2.000** on ship and ferry
8 border crosses
61 fuel tanks
5 flat tyres
1 fall down
0 damage
2 changes of front tyre
3 changes of rear tyre
28 hotels and lodges
12 earthquake replicas

41° hottest day
-3° coldest day
1 wheel "baptized" by two foxes' pee
11 frigates in the Strait of Magellan
20.845 photographs taken for this book
68 DVDs for back up
3 whales (seen during sightseeing)
1.000 guanacos
2 Cordillera crosses at **4.300** meters

Fitz Roy, Darwin & Napoleón

Following Charles Darwin's tracks through Argentina, Chile and Uruguay, I came across dozens of places named after our protagonists. I am not referring to the geographical features baptized by the Beagle crew members, or in honour of them. I am talking about something else: from street names in Buenos Aires to sophisticated hotels in Chile; the Darwin-FitzRoy duet is once and again repeated. But one stood out from the rest. The last day which was dedicated to the island of Chiloé, we traveled with the GS from Castro to Cucao. I was interested in seeing how much the muddy road Darwin described as tortuous and impassable had changed. Besides, the place that has today become a natural reserve is still home to the descendants of the natives Charles met in 1834. I got there easily, through a paved and quaint road, but with evident signs of clearing in its surroundings. Cucao is small, but of a striking beauty. Despite the 50 kilometers that separate it from Castro, it is inhospitable and not well-known. About 400 people live there. One of them is a German woman, Susi Daum. Together with her Chilote husband (born and raised in Chiloé), they run the Charles Darwin lodging house, a few meters away from the National Park's entrance.

If the English scientist lived, I am sure he would stay there during his holidays, off Down House, where he lived.

My journey was only beginning. The odometer marked 4.760 kilometers since my departure from Buenos Aires. But meeting Susi was a sign of good omen of what was to come. It wasn't a high season for tourism and the Lodge was closed. However, they invited me to visit it. A special aroma enticed me and I doubted whether I should keep going or convince them to let me stay. I asked Susi what she was cooking, and with a guffaw she answered it was Napoleon's (her favourite pig) lunch. They have many animals as pets, amongst them a chubby one who weighs 150 kilos and who responds to the orders imparted in German and gets home-made food as a reward. I climbed my GS and promised to return. I hope I can fulfill my promise.

For reservations contact *paradordarwin@hotmail.com*. You won't regret it! ∎

Bibliography

As I told you in the preface, many books and articles have aided my research to understand this story:

National Geographic
Issues of December 2008 and February 2009.

Darwin, La historia de un hombre extraordinario
Tim Berra. Tusquets Editores

Diario de viajes de un naturalista alrededor del mundo
Charles Darwin. Elefante Blanco.

Hacia los confines del mundo
Harry Thompson. Ediciones Salamandra.

Viajes del Adventure y el Beagle I y II
Robert FitzRoy. Zagier & Urruty Publications.

La traición de Darwin
Gerardo Bartolomé. Zagier & Urruty Publications.

From so simple a beginning
The Four Great Books of Charles Darwin
Charles Darwin, edited by E.O. Wilson.
W.W. Norton & Company.

A narrative of the voyage of H.M.S. Beagle
The Folio Society.

Darwin
John van Wyhe. Andre Deutsch/Carlton Publishing G.

Darwin y los fueguinos
Arnoldo Canclini. Zagier & Urruty Publications.

Diario de la Patagonia
Charles Darwin. Ediciones Continente.

Pedro Sarmiento de Gamboa
Rosa Arciniega. Editorial Sudamericana.

Viaje alrededor del mundo
L-A de Bougainville. Eudeba.

Autobiografía
Charles Darwin. Grupo Editorial Norma.

Darwin
Sir J. Huxley & H.D.B Kettlewel. Salvat Editores.

Rosas, aportes para su historia
Ernesto Celesia. Ediciones Peuser.

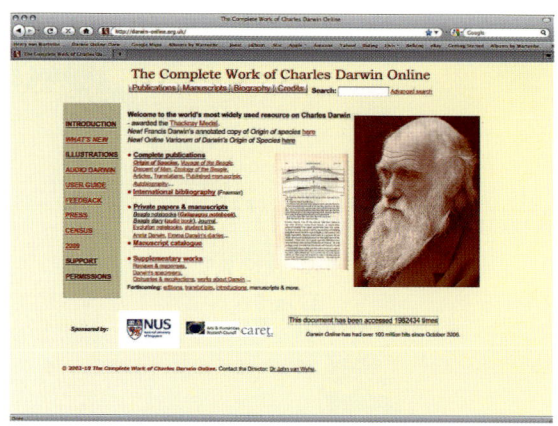

The computer and Internet have been of great help. Thanks to programmes as Google Earth, I could check the coordinates for every destination of this trip. I also surfed many webpages looking for information; and fortunately found an allied of valuable assistance that let me use texts and prints: http://darwin-online.org.uk

The site (directed by doctor John van Wyhe) carries absolutely everything about Darwin: the books published by Darwin and FitzRoy, the journals and original notes, the documents, the sketches and drawings, prints and letters... In association with Cambridge University and other important entities they keep Darwin's legacy in use. The site —created in 2002— has had more tan a hundred million visits in the last four years.

Acknowledgements

I started dreaming about this book in 2009, while I was shooting *Autos Clásicos en Argentina*.
By February 2010 –the countdown to start the trip was already running– I had to plan our family holidays without distracting me from the project. As I was going on tour March 4th, my aim was to spend as much time as possible with my wife and my daughters.

We stayed for two weeks at Anita Rusconi's farm (and her son Juan) in Punta del Este. The house is imposing, all made of stone, a pharaonic building (ordered by Luis Rusconi to arquitect Horacio Ravazzani) that demanded two years to be constructed.
One day I asked our host where the stone was from and she answered me:
–*From the hills of Minas.*
Minas was one of my destinations, as Darwin had been there almost two hundred years ago. I am sure our friend Charles stood on one of the thousand of stones that erected these huge walls...! Aren't you?

This list may be incomplete.

There are so many people that made this book possible. To begin with, my wife and my daughters: **Dolores, Mia y Amélie**. To them, my everlasting gratitude.

Raúl y Dolores, my parents in law, were always focused on solving any problem during my absence and especially holding back the little ones. They were a good support!

To all the people of the trail, who –without noticing it– were a company during my *solitaire* expedition.

The book would not exist without the sponsors. I am very grateful to all of them, but it is fair to mention the aid of **Ezequiel Eskenazi** (YPF), **Christian Menges** (BMW) y **Martín de Carabassa** (Rev'it!). They said 'Yes' before asking me what I would do. In the meantime, friends as **Vanesa Kreth** o **Alfredo Fierro** (British Embassy) were already casting new contacts. The Museo Naval de Tigre (the Navy Museum), his chairman **Captain Horacio Molina Pico**, the museologist **Pablo Pereyra** and the librarian **Elisa Collazo**. They allowed me to consult and take pictures of the log of H.M.S. Beagle, a 'jewel' of their own; very well kept by the museum. A priceless incunabulum!

Raúl Podetti and his **Proyecto Experience!** He added information and advice, and gave the video of his play "La Aventura del Beagle" (The Beagle Adventure) to go with the limited edition of the book.

The assitance of **Gerardo Bartolomé** has been essential. He provided me with accurate information and coordinates. In the logistics, **Willy Rodríguez** together with **Ezequiel Huergo** and **Nico Sansalone**.

To my cousin **Mary Vigil**, who was my guardian angel all the way through sms.

I could always speak on the phone due to **Twiins**, the bluetooth microphone for the helmet.

The Hoopla team, headed by **Guiye Ensinck**, responsible for the blog (www.darwinalsurdelsur.com.ar).

Fernando Bravo and **Alfredo Leuco** interviewed me for their programme of Continental Radio. They mentioned my blog and in few days only the number of visits was impressing. Same happened with **Gato Barbery** and **Nacho El-Haiek** and their tv shows. I also would like to thank La Nación newspaper and Gente magazine. **Jorge de Luján Gutiérrez** put me through to the Argentine Armada. Captain **Daniel Ramallo**, of the press office and captains **Leonard** (chief of Agr. Lanchas Rápidas) and **Buscarolo** (commander of

A.R.A. Intrépida) made possible my visit to Good Success Bay in the extreme of Tierra del Fuego.

Juan Carlos Varela (Australis Cruises) did not hesitate to embark me to Cape Horn. The staff of Oro Fueguino Lodge in Punta Arenas made me feel at home. **Dinka** and **Peyo**: thank you so much!

I met many people through my webpage, but I'd like to point out Romana Areco's permanent contribution. She hosted me at hotel Los Alamos, where I got my strength back, and also found a home for the BMW in Río Gallegos.

María del Carmen Peretti and **Miguel Schlegel**, very faithful fans. My thanks to all of the followers, some are lifelong friends, others new company:

Fernando Márquez, Martín Huergo, Cristián Trepat, Ricardo Zapata, 6th and 7th form of School N° 6157, Walter Acevedo, Juan Carlos Belcastro, Guillermo and Víctor Clement. And to everyone who sent comments (the page had more than 6 thousand visits!).

I gave many lectures in different schools. I'd like to thank librarian **Patricia López** (San Carlos College in San Lorenzo) for her help.

I had a wonderful stay at Faro San Isidro (San Isidro Lighthouse). **Sandra Barahona** and **Marcelo Arratia**, and a friend of them **Ana María Piffoault**, made me feel that the End of the World was like home.

The five consecutive flat tyres (with the motorcycle) were also unforgettable. I visited many tyre fixers, but only one –in Natales Port– found out what the problem was. I regret not having his name; the store is very near (150 meters) hotel Charles Darwin. Thanks, buddy!

Alberto Yunis (El Rincón) and **Matilde Wilson** (La Aurora) both openned their "tranqueras" and let me take pictures of unique places. **Federico Bonomi** made my last stop perfect in Punta Gorda and **Martín De Ferrari** (Danone) guided me in Villavicencio, Mendoza. And there's something special I'd like to mention of Mendoza. As Darwin did, I knocked on many friends'doors to stay overnight. At Finca La Anita, in Luján de Cuyo, **Antonio** and **Manuel Mas** –together with **Norma**– gave this project the lucky winds to succeed. What begins well, finishes at its best! This trip was like a revenge for us (they know exactly why).
To all of you,